T0355004

STOP
LETTING YOUR PAST
CONTROL YOU

STOP

LETTING YOUR PAST
CONTROL YOU

A step-by-step guide
to becoming who you want to be

D R .   B I L L   O ' L E A R Y

Archway Publishing books may be ordered through booksellers or by contacting:

Archway Publishing
1663 Liberty Drive
Bloomington, IN 47403
www.archwaypublishing.com
844-669-3957

ISBN: 978-1-6657-7197-9 (sc)
ISBN: 978-1-6657-7198-6 (e)

Library of Congress Control Number: 2025900745

Print information available on the last page.

Archway Publishing rev. date: 03/06/2025

Contents

About the Author

Dr. Bill O'Leary, PsyD

Bill has been active in the mental health field since 1991. He initially worked at residential and psychiatric facilities for emotionally disturbed adolescents. During that time, he began working with adolescent offenders. In 1999, he received his MSW from Adelphi University and began his own consulting business named People Talk, Inc. Through consulting, Bill has taught for SUNY Stony Brook, Fordham University, Buffalo State, as well as helping rookies for the New York Giants, and thousands of students through bullying and sexual harassment workshops in schools. Bill has also taught for NY City ACS, specializing in Common Core, sexual abuse, and child protective investigations. He as also served as a first responder in local fire departments since 2000.

Currently, he teaches on a consultant basis, is a media consultant, a NY State board member for professionals working to prevent sexual abuse, and works extensively as a forensic psychologist with law enforcement cases. For over thirty years, he has been committed to helping people address their issues and evolve into their ideal self. He is interviewed frequently by newspapers and news stations to discuss issues such as bullying, parenting, abuse, and violent crimes.

Bill's most important and rewarding role has been as a husband to his amazing and supportive wife, Christine, and father to his two incredible and talented sons, Logan and Dylan.

Foreword

There are a number of books that focus on dealing with past issues. The common themes seem to be forgiveness and acceptance. While these messages are a necessary part of the process, they aren't very practical. Forgiving someone is cathartic and often makes the forgiver feel better about themselves, but they can't effectively use it to overcome the underlying issues.

There is also a sense of an afflicter and a victim. Readers should not have to feel like victims because they've been hurt in the past. They should be able to see hurt as normal, but something that is given far too much power. Healing is possible and moving on is possible.

This book will empower the reader right from the beginning. You will see what you have been avoiding for most of your life and that by picking up this book, you have chosen to be the one in power and control. By applying the exercises in the book, you will finally take control of your life's direction.

Conspicuously missing from other books are tangible skills one can walk away with. This book will have actual exercises you can use to start improving your life immediately. There will be short-term and long-term goals that provide present as well as future benefits.

Introduction

If you are looking to take control of your life and work towards your full potential as a person, then you've picked up the right book. *Stop Letting the Past Control You* is a labor of love developed over decades of working with people and the human condition. I've been working in a forensic environment since the early 1990s, giving me a unique perspective on people and how the mind works. I've had the honor of having people let me into their minds and their most personal thoughts. As a result, I've seen painful experiences turn into very dark actions and, at times, inspire strength. I've learned that everyone experiences things differently, which is why I've learned not to say, "I know exactly how you feel." I don't. Even if we experienced the same exact thing, we experienced it differently.

Every single person has their own unique experiences that can only be gleaned by walking through someone's life. This is done by hearing their life story. Each person's life story is like a book. To try to understand someone based on a portion of their life would be like reading one chapter of a book and then writing a synopsis and review of the whole book. It is just not possible. We don't need to understand everyone on that level, but we should, at least, understand ourselves. If we look at our lives like a book, then we can see that the earlier chapters influence the later ones. Since we are still alive, our book is still being written. By gaining insight into ourselves, we can decide to write our book instead of having parts written for us.

This book will help you reflect on your past so you can understand how it has affected you thus far. This means there are already great things you utilize now that are derived from your life experiences. It may, and usually does, also mean there are negative things that you say, feel, and do that are results of your experiences as well. Before today, you may not have been aware of them. After today, you won't be able to blame them on your past. One of my new favorite sayings is that we need to be stronger than our excuses. Hopefully, reading this book means you're ready to face and overcome that challenge.

Chapter 1

WHY SHOULD YOU
CONFRONT YOUR PAST?

"You can have results or excuses. Not both"
– Arnold Schwarzenegger

The concept of dragging our past with us is universal, and in many ways, this is great. We are shaped by our experiences, they make us who we are. My wife, Christine, and I often look at pictures over the years and reflect and smile. Photos are such a great way to keep our past with us. Smells, songs, movies, and even thoughts also bring us back to earlier times. It's great to recapture those moments when they are positive memories. Bad memories are not so good. Sure, they are part of our history, but they can be difficult for many. This concept will be explored further when we discuss the emotional continuum.

This book digs to the core of who we are and who we want to be. It's a life-changing journey towards cutting out the bad, expanding on the good, and being the best version of ourselves. Since we are influenced from our past, it is important to be honest and aware of how we are influenced and choose how we want to be influenced.

One of the first things I ask people who come to me from jail is why they did what they did to get themselves locked up. The answer is usually that they were under the influence of drugs or alcohol, or they had bad experiences as a child. They often don't know. I then ask them how they would know what to fix without knowing the underlying reasons. If we truly want growth, we have to be willing to do the work. It's not difficult work, conceptually, but it does make us face uncomfortable truths.

We're all capable of doing "bad" things. In fact, we all do "bad" things in some form or another. Saying this doesn't make it okay, but it is a reality. Some people do some really bad or unusual things. People ask me all the time, "Why do people do these things?" The answer, for all of us, is simple. We do what we do because we want to. This is a very honest and empowering statement. If we can take ownership of our actions, we can work to change them. The first step is answering one simple question honestly: What is the reason I wanted to do that?

People often mistake excuses for reasons. The excuse usually has to do with simple disempowering statements such as "that's what I learned when I was growing up" or "that's just who I am." That would be fine if they were reasons for good choices. Unfortunately, these statements are usually used as excuses for bad choices. In some ways, it is honest to say we do things because that's what we learned. This could have to do with actual lessons taught to us or ways we learned to cope due to various experiences. This book will explore a number of life experiences where people may learn maladaptive coping skills.

We usually don't blame children for their bad choices if we see they came from bad situations. In fact, we are often sad that they have been exposed to bad things and are more understanding if they "act out". If a ten-year-old girl is sexually abused and acts out sexually, we feel bad for her and don't see it as her fault. If that same girl reaches nineteen and becomes a stripper, we often look down at her or see her as a sexual object. We don't see her as that ten-year-old girl still acting out her abuse. At what age do we start seeing someone as accountable? If she somehow got help at ten, would she still be stripping at nineteen? Is her abuse as a child a reason or an excuse? These are difficult questions that I will attempt to answer later in the book.

Confrontation

We'll start with our first mini-exercise. Write the word "confrontation" on a piece of paper. Now, write down the words that come to mind as you look at the word. Take a moment to reflect on this before continuing reading.

I'm guessing the words were predominantly negative. Some of the common words that people think of are fight, argument, yelling. What does it really mean to confront something? It means to address it. If we don't address things, how can we hope to correct or improve them? Confrontation is great. It's how we improve and grow. After all, nothing changes if nothing changes. The trick is to confront things in a way that facilitates change. This means we need to think about what we want to change and how to do that effectively.

Dealing with our past can be a scary concept for many people. I've had many patients say, "I'm okay, but I don't want to talk about my past." That statement is usually an indicator that they are not okay. It's natural to want to avoid addressing pain. It's a similar excuse people use to avoid going to the doctor when something hurts. It is a good self-check though. If we can't talk about it, there's probably something to address.

If we don't confront these issues, we carry them with us. In carrying them, we are often weighed down by them. These issues also influence our current thoughts, emotions, and actions in ways we can't even calculate. Think of the example above, not only are the girl's actions impacted, so are her thoughts, feelings, relationships, self-worth, and a number of other possible areas.

There's a very popular approach in psychology called cognitive behavioral therapy (CBT). CBT is a short-term, goal-oriented psychotherapy treatment that takes a hands-on, practical approach to problem-solving. Its goal is to change the patterns of thinking or behavior that are behind people's difficulties, and so change the way they feel. It is used to help treat a wide range of issues in a person's life, from sleeping difficulties or relationship problems, to drug and alcohol abuse or anxiety and depression. CBT works by changing people's attitudes and their behavior by focusing on the thoughts, images, beliefs, and attitudes that are held (a person's cognitive processes), and how these processes relate to the way a person behaves and deals with emotional problems.

An important advantage of CBT is that it tends to be short, taking five to ten months for most emotional problems. Clients attend one session per week, each session lasting approximately 50 minutes. During this time, the client and therapist work together to understand what the problems are and develop new strategies for tackling them. CBT introduces patients to a set of principles that they can apply whenever they need to, and that will last them a lifetime.

CBT can be thought of as a combination of psychotherapy and behavioral therapy. Psychotherapy emphasizes the importance of the personal meaning we place on things and how thinking patterns begin in childhood. Behavioral therapy pays close attention to the relationship between our problems, our behavior, and our thoughts. Most psychotherapists who practice CBT personalize and customize the therapy to the specific needs and personality of each patient.

Some History on CBT

CBT was invented by psychiatrist Aaron Beck in the 1960s. He was doing psychoanalysis at the time and observed that his patients tended to have an internal dialogue going on in their minds during his analytical sessions–almost as if they were talking to themselves. But they would only report a fraction of this kind of thinking to him.

For example, in a therapy session, the client might be thinking to herself: "He (the therapist) hasn't said much today. I wonder if he's annoyed with me?" These thoughts might make the client feel slightly anxious or perhaps annoyed. She could then respond to this thought with a further thought: "He's probably tired, or perhaps I haven't been talking about the most important things." The second thought might change how the client was feeling.

Beck realized that the link between thoughts and feelings was critical. He invented the term automatic thoughts to describe emotion-filled thoughts that might pop up in the mind. Beck found that people weren't always fully aware of such thoughts, but they could learn to identify and report them. If a person was feeling upset in some way, the thoughts were usually negative and neither realistic nor helpful. Beck found that identifying these thoughts was the key to the client understanding and overcoming his or her difficulties.

Beck called it cognitive therapy because of the importance it places on thinking. It's now known as cognitive behavioral therapy (CBT) because the therapy employs behavioral techniques as well. The balance between the cognitive and the behavioral elements varies among the different therapies of this type, but all come under the umbrella term cognitive behavior therapy. CBT has since undergone successful scientific trials in many places by different teams, and it has been applied to a wide variety of problems.

CBT is based on a model or theory that it's not events themselves that upset us, but the meanings we give them. If our thoughts are too negative, it can block us seeing things or doing things that don't fit—that disconfirm—with what we believe is true. In other words, we continue to hold on to the same old thoughts and fail to learn anything new.

For example, a depressed woman may think, "I can't face going into work today: I can't do it. Nothing will go right. I'll feel awful." As a result of having these thoughts—and of believing them—she may well call in sick. By behaving like this, she won't have the chance to find out that her prediction was wrong. She might have found some things she could do, and at least some things that were okay. But, instead, she stays at home, brooding about her failure to go in and ends up thinking: "I've let everyone down. They will be angry with me. Why can't I do what everyone else does? I'm so weak and useless." That woman probably ends up feeling worse, and has even more difficulty going in to work the next day. Thinking, behaving, and feeling like this may start a downward spiral. This vicious circle can apply to many different kinds of problems.

Beck suggested that these thinking patterns are set up in childhood, and they become automatic and relatively fixed. So, a child who didn't get much open affection from their parents but was praised for school work, might come to think, "I have to do well all the time. If I don't, people will reject me." Such a rule for living (known as a dysfunctional assumption) may do well for the person a lot of the time and help them to work hard. But if something happens that's beyond their control and they experience failure, then the dysfunctional thought pattern may be triggered. The person may then begin to have automatic thoughts like, "I've completely failed. No one will like me. I can't face them."

CBT acts to help the person understand that this is what's going on. It helps him or her to step outside their automatic thoughts and test them out. CBT would encourage the depressed woman mentioned earlier to examine real-life experiences to see what happens to her, or to others, in similar situations. Then, in the light of a more realistic perspective, she may be able to take the chance of testing out what other people think, by revealing something of her difficulties to friends.

Clearly, negative things can and do happen. But when we are in a disturbed state of mind, we may be basing our predictions and interpretations on a biased view of the situation, making the difficulty that we face seem much worse. CBT helps people to correct these misinterpretations. This concept is critical to maximize your ability to process your thoughts and influence your actions.

It's really quite simple. Our thoughts come first, then feelings, and then our behaviors. Which one do we have the most control over? Luckily, the answer is our thoughts. If we accept that we control our thoughts, then we are on our way to controlling our feelings and behaviors. You've probably heard the saying, "Change your thoughts, change your world." It stems from this concept. If we think positively, we will feel positive, and then we will make positive choices. The opposite is also true. In short, if you don't like the way you are feeling, then change the way you are thinking.

Needs

We all have needs, and these needs often drive our behaviors in life. But what does it mean to need something? It means we can't do without it. We have to have it. On the other hand, there is want. We may want something, but not need it. This is an important distinction because we weigh wants and needs differently. It's okay to want something, and meeting our wants contributes to our happiness. Meeting wants can be a slippery slope as some of our wants can compromise our values, relationships, and freedoms. Meeting wants usually involves some sort of cost analysis. It can be as simple as I want ice cream, but I also value my health. How much ice cream is okay to have, and how much compromises my health or fitness goals?

There are two ways to look at needs. The first is probably the one you're most familiar with–Maslow's Hierarchy of Needs. Abraham Maslow, a humanistic psychologist, contextualized the meeting of needs in the form of a pyramid. Maslow posits that we have more basic needs that must be met before we can look to meet higher level needs. The one we all seek at first is the category of basic/physiological needs. These are biological requirements for human survival, e.g., air, food, drink, shelter, clothing, warmth, sex, sleep. It would certainly be difficult to focus on other things when one is worried about these items. Therefore, our behaviors are basically focused on efforts to attain them.

Once people's physiological requirements are met, the next need that arises is a safe environment. Our safety needs are apparent even early in childhood, as children have a need for safe and predictable environments and typically react with fear or anxiety when these are not met. As adults, efforts to feel safe often show up via defense mechanisms, as outlined by Sigmund Freud. Defense mechanisms are unconscious strategies whereby people protect themselves from anxious thoughts or feelings. They can be used to defend negative thoughts or actions, but they can also allow people to navigate painful experiences. Safety is a strong motivator for why people take out medical and homeowners insurance.

According to Maslow, the next need in the hierarchy involves feeling loved and accepted. This need includes both romantic relationships as well as ties to friends and family members. It also includes our need to feel that we belong to a social group. Importantly, this need encompasses both feeling loved and feeling love towards others.

The next need is self-esteem. Esteem needs involve the desire to feel good about ourselves. According to Maslow, esteem needs include two components. The first involves feeling self-confidence and feeling good about oneself. The second component involves feeling valued by others; that is, feeling that our achievements and contributions have been recognized by other people. When people's esteem needs are met, they feel confident and see their contributions and achievements as valuable and important.

The last need is self-actualization. This refers to feeling fulfilled, or feeling that we are living up to our potential. One unique feature of self-actualization is that it looks different for everyone. For one person, self-actualization might involve helping others; for another person, it might involve achievements in an artistic or creative field. Essentially, self-actualization means feeling that we are doing what we believe we are meant to do. According to Maslow, achieving self-actualization is not common. However, Maslow describes peak experiences of self-actualization as often fleeting.

Maslow's model is a great systematic model for understanding human behavior and how to assess it. There is a potential drawback in trying to understand behavior in a hierarchical approach versus a linear or open one. Another model of needs is very similar but it takes a more open approach in that it looks at all behavior as an attempt to get needs met without the restriction of the hierarchy. If we take Maslow's needs and just say all behavior functions to meet our needs, then we can then just ask, "What need is this behavior satisfying?" This is an important question in understanding why we do what we do and how to change it.

This model sets a foundation for self-reflection as well as understanding others. Our negative behaviors are attached to our needs. If we have to get our needs met, it is important to look at positive behaviors over negative behaviors. An easy example is smoking cigarettes. Smoking is a behavior that meets different needs for different people. For many, smoking is a stress relief, which can be linked to safety or self-esteem. If one wants to stop smoking, they would need to find an alternative behavior that would meet those same needs. If they don't, quitting would be much more difficult. Of course, this is a lot easier said than done.

Time For Change

Exploring the role of needs is a piece of a bigger picture that brings us to the Change Model. I was introduced to the Change Model when I was a trainer at the Administration for Children's Services Academy in New York City. It's a great model that we all unconsciously apply all the time. Since it's unconscious, we are limited in how well we use it. Let's start by thinking about a behavior that you've changed at some point. If you changed it, it's because you didn't like that you did it. That means that you were uncomfortable about doing it. Present discomfort is the first element and it's a really good thing. It's the start to change. If we were comfortable, then there would be no reason to change anything.

The next element (and the most difficult) is emotional security. This refers to the belief that we can still get our needs met in the form of another behavior. As discussed earlier, we behave to get our needs met. To feel emotionally secure, we have to feel that we can replace the behavior with something else and still feel that we won't be missing something. When you changed your behavior, you replaced it with something else. What was it? What need did it meet? You may not have realized it, but you changed how you got that need met and it worked. If it didn't, you'd be back to the same old behavior. When it comes to other behaviors that you don't like, you just might not have found a viable replacement behavior.

The third element is internalization of responsibility. It's a wordy way of saying you own it. If you don't own your behaviors, then you externalize responsibility, or blame. Blaming others is one of the most disempowering things we can do. It gives power to other people to control us, even if they're not trying to. When we own our problems, we have the power to fix them.

The fourth element is efficacy. This is the belief that you are capable of successfully stopping the behavior. The key word here is belief. If you can, but don't believe you can, then you won't. It's one of the key messages from the Ted Lasso show. A great example of how this works is the Little Engine That Could. His belief got him up the hill. He believed he had the ability, which led to his success.

The last element is a preferred alternative future. This element relies on belief as well. It's a vision of the end goal, what it looks like, and that it's possible to get there. You know what you want to change and what will be different when you do. If you didn't have a behavior in mind when we started this piece, I encourage you to think of one now and reread this part. It's a really important component to grasp before moving forward. Once you've done that, we're going to look at how to use this consciously.

So, now that we have the five elements, what do we do with them? The step to that question is easy. You see which ones are high and which are low. I know that sounds confusing, so picture having five gas tanks and a gauge for each. Each element is a tank. The fuller they are, the better. For this to work, all of the tanks must have enough fuel in them. For the change to occur, each tank has to have enough fuel. Now, think of a behavior that you would like to change. This is important, so make sure you have one in mind.

One or more of your tanks are low and we must identify them. How do I know? Because you're still doing the behavior. This means you're resistant to changing it. That resistance is caused by your low tanks, so we have to identify them. We can figure it out with some questions. Are you uncomfortable? If so, on a scale of 1 (not very) to 10 (very), how uncomfortable are you? Anything under a six means you're still comfortable with doing the behavior.

What needs are you meeting by doing the behavior? Can you think of a different behavior that will meet the same needs? On a scale of 1 to 10, how confident are you that the new behavior will work? This question is to assess for emotional security. Whose fault is it that you behave like this? If it's yours, that's great. That means you can do something about it. If it's someone else's fault, then you are powerless to change it until it's yours. How confident are you in your ability to change the behavior? Use the same scale of 1 to 10. Lastly, how solid is your vision of what things will be like once you've changed the behavior?

For each element, you should have a number from 1 to 10. Each one under six identifies your resistance areas. Each one over five is your power area. So far, we've completed step one–assessing change readiness. We don't have to do much with the power elements. We just need to focus on the resistance ones and work towards promoting change readiness. Essentially, we need to add fuel to the low tanks. Here are some tips for each one:

Present discomfort: Your sense of discomfort with the present situation. Present discomfort is generally associated with an unmet need. Throughout this process, it's important to think about what need or needs our behavior is meeting. Since it's good to be uncomfortable, we must make ourselves okay with not being okay with the behavior.

Emotional security: A state in which an individual believes that personal physical safety, attachments, identity, trust in others, and autonomy are not threatened while the individual is engaged in the change process. It is the basis of the willingness to risk, to trust, and to form meaningful relationships. Emotional security is linked to our behavior meeting our needs. Whether negative or positive, our behaviors meet our needs. Since needs are something we can't do without, it's essential to know that we can find a positive behavior to replace a negative one. If we can't, we are more likely to stay with or go back to the negative one.

Internalization of responsibility: The extent to which an individual accepts personal responsibility for his or her actions and needs. This element reflects the individual's understanding of their role in getting his or her needs met and/or creating problems for self or others. Ultimately, if we own our problems, we can fix them. If we blame other people for our problems, we are powerless to fix them. Since this is difficult at times, it's important to look at what our role is in the behavior. Other people may play a role as well, but we need to focus on our own since that is all we will have direct control over.

Efficacy: The confidence or belief in one's power or ability to produce desired results. Efficacy is an interesting concept as it is not just based on whether the person has the ability, but that they believe that they do. Efficacy can be weakened when someone has attempted to change the behavior and the past and was not successful. Sisyphus must have been exhausted trying to get the rock up the mountain, but he kept trying, as he believed in his ability to succeed. When looking at this element, it's important to look at other ways to change the behavior if what we've tried didn't work before. Otherwise, we're just living the definition of insanity.

Preferred alternative future: The vision of something different–a goal or changed state of relationships, conditions, and behavior patterns– for which one can strive. Preferred alternative future is based on a person's ability to imagine that their needs could be satisfied in the new situation resulting from their changes. It is also linked to culture, self-concept, experience, and values. It's easy to snowball here and start to feel hopeless. It's important to remain optimistic and really visualize what will be different and how that will look as it pertains to the behavior.

I'll illustrate the model based on a behavior I changed before even knowing anything about it. At the time, I was 27, so it was quite a while back. The behavior I changed was giving the finger and cursing when I was driving. It's something I only did when driving and hadn't given it much thought. This was especially relevant as I'm not big on cursing and pride myself on being calm in situations and not one to react to people by giving the finger.

My wife and I were dating at the time, and we drove to Ocean City, Maryland for our first trip away together. We had a great time and were getting ready to drive back to New York. She said she would drive. I thought she meant the first half of the drive, but she said she'd rather drive the whole way as it was uncomfortable when I drove down to Maryland since I cursed. Naturally, I defended the behavior and said it was a stressful drive based on a work crisis before we left and heavy rain conditions on the way. She said I do it other times as well–which was true. I said that I would drive and wouldn't curse, since it made her uncomfortable and I really didn't like that I did it in the first place.

Not far into the drive, someone drove in a way that annoyed me and I called them a douchebag (I'm not proud of it, but that's what happened). I felt her look at me and defended the word by saying it's not a curse. It's a hygiene product, like a toothbrush. I'm not very versed in the use of them, so my argument was weak. She said it's not the same thing as a toothbrush. I asked if "toothbrush" was "comfortable" since the other word wasn't. She said sure, so I called people toothbrush instead. When calling someone a toothbrush, since it's such a random word, it's difficult to stay angry.

Here we are many years later, and I still don't curse or give the finger when driving. If I did it for Christine, I would only make the change when driving with her, as it wouldn't be fair to continue it knowing it made her uncomfortable. Instead, I did it for me, since it conflicted with my values for myself. This change happened organically, but can be tapped into in order to consciously make changes in the future. Let's walk through the elements of change here.

Step one: Assessing change readiness

I must have been low in at least one area, since it was a behavior I had been doing. Prior to changing the behavior, present discomfort was probably about a five. This was due to justifying it, but not being uncomfortable enough to change it. Emotional security was around a four, in that I got something out of it. In reflecting, it may have been my one curse area. I also felt offended by the actions of other drivers and felt justified in reacting to them.

I blamed other people for my actions, so I must have been low in internalization of responsibility. In terms of efficacy, I think it was closer to a ten. I didn't see it as something I couldn't change, just something I hadn't bothered to. The last element is preferred alternative future. I hadn't thought about this one either, but wouldn't have seen it as hopeless. If I had thought of it, it would have been high, as it would just be driving without being as affected by how other people were driving.

Step two: Promoting change readiness

At the time, I was above a six in efficacy and preferred alternative future. The other three were below a six. Present discomfort was immediately raised by confronting the hypocrisy of my actions. I don't like cursing or reacting with anger, yet I was doing it. By facing that contradiction, I was quickly uncomfortable. Blaming other people for my actions is another hypocrisy. If we own our choices, then we have the power to change them. This was another easy self-confrontation.

Emotional security is usually the toughest one. In this case, I felt giving the finger or cursing was a way to assert myself to the other drivers. It felt good to lash out in some way at someone who I believed was wronging me. Overall, I know nothing about the other person or why they are behaving the way they are. I was personalizing something that wasn't personal. Even worse, I was letting their actions influence how I felt and how I behaved. By using CBT, I was able to change my perception of the situation, which changes how I experience it. I also like to feel happy, not upset, and that simple thought change made that possible. It also built my emotional security to be more congruent with my values.

So, let's put it all together and change something. We'll begin with assessing change readiness. You'll need your notebook for this one. Identify something you do that you don't like. This one should be easy since you're picking it.

What don't you like about the behavior? How does it negatively affect you or those around you? On a scale of 1 to 10, how uncomfortable are you with that behavior?

What need is being met by the behavior? What would happen if you stopped the behavior? What are some other behaviors you could do that would meet the same need? On a scale of 1 to 10, how likely do you think the positive behavior is to work?

Who do you believe has responsibility for this situation? In what ways are you responsible for this situation? On a scale of 1 to 10, how much responsibility do you have?

What have you tried to do about this concern in the past? How successful have you been in making changes in other areas of your life? On a scale of 1 to 10, how capable do you think you are of changing the behavior?

What's your picture of an ideal solution to this situation? What needs of yours could be met if things were different? On a scale of 1 to 10, how possible do you think the change is?

As we've discussed, your low number elements are holding you back. Now that you know which elements to focus on, you can work on those areas to reduce your resistance. Since you identified the behavior, there should be a decent degree of discomfort (otherwise, why pick it?). If your Emotional security is low, it's really important to focus on positive replacement behaviors. If you're struggling on your own, ask someone you feel comfortable with for suggestions.

If internalization of responsibility is low, it's crucial to focus on your locus of control and apply that to what power you have concerning the problem behavior. This is only about you, no one else. If your efficacy is low, think about tougher problems you've solved or endured. It's helpful to realize we've overcome difficulties before–this is doable. If preferred alternative future is low, focus on the rewards of the change. We can easily be lost in a cycle when we know what we are doing is negative and feel worse because we aren't making the effort to change it. Remember, thought and perspective are some of the few things we actually have control over. Belief in that knowledge is very powerful.

You have now learned and practiced one of the best tools to change anything about yourself that you want. You have also had success in using it many times without even knowing it. Before now, you used it unconsciously, but now you can use it consciously, which means you can use it deliberately and more effectively. You are now ready for one more concept before we close out the chapter.

The Stages of Learning

The last part of our foundation is exploring how we learn. This is important as we learn better when we realize that we are always students. According to Socrates, true wisdom is knowing we know nothing. That philosophy should keep us forever developing our ability to learn and grow. There are four stages to learning. We are all at every stage depending on what skill we are talking about.

The first stage is to be unconsciously unskilled. This means that we don't know that we don't know. This stage can be the most dangerous and frustrating to others. If someone is unconsciously unskilled, they are more likely to attempt tasks despite the possible risks in doing so. It's very unpleasant to work with someone at this stage as they are unwilling to learn and will often tell you that what you're doing is wrong. You definitely don't want to be that person, but we probably all have been at some points.

The second stage is to be consciously unskilled. This isn't as bad as it sounds. It means that we know that we don't know, and that means we can be willing and able to learn. It also suggests that we can refrain from doing something wrong, or possibly dangerous, until we have more knowledge or skill. This stage can feel bad, but as we learned, discomfort can be a great catalyst for change.

The next stage is to be consciously skilled. This means we know what we know. We are skilled, know what works, and why it works. We can be consistent in results and impart those skills onto others. This is an especially important stage for supervisors when training others.

The last stage is to be unconsciously skilled. This means that we don't necessarily know what we know. We can do the task well without having to think about what we're doing. Hopefully, we were able to move towards this stage when we worked on the change piece.

This book strives to promote these stages in a number of areas as we go on. A lot of what is discussed in the book will be familiar to you and is organized in a way that allows you to apply it better in your life. The trick is to be honest with yourself about what stage of learning you're in, depending on what skill you're focusing on. It's easy to think you've got it and don't need to work on it. That way of thinking can lead to stagnation or lack of growth. No matter how good someone is at a skill, we can only grow by conceding that we can still do better.

Now that we have a foundation of concepts and skills, we are going to open ourselves up to looking inside and backwards to really understand ourselves. Once we do that, we will look at how possible instances of abuse, substance abuse, sexual abuse, and parenting have affected us in ways and how we can change that. Naturally, some areas will speak more to you than others, as we have all had different experiences. You may not relate to some of the issues personally, but don't just breeze through them. Unfortunately, all of these types of abuses are too common in society, so you probably have people in your life that know them well. This will help you gain insight into them and may help you support them. At the very least, you can pass this book on to them. The book will move us to a new level of healing and enable you to decide who and how you want to be moving forward.

Chapter 2

SIGNS THAT THE PAST IS CONTROLLING YOU

See, when you drive home today, you've got a big windshield
on the front of your car. And you've got a little bitty rearview
mirror. And the reason the windshield is so large and the
rearview mirror is so small is because what's happened in your
past is not near as important as what's in your future.
- Joel Osteen

Very few of us go through life without some type of hurt. It's a lot more universal than people realize. Sadly, many people suffer silently for way too long. Often, this is partly due to feeling like no one else has been through it or that no one would understand. The longer one goes without speaking about it, the harder it can be to bring it up. As a result, the damage can last a lot longer than people even realize. The negative effects can even change form to the point that we don't even realize they're connected.

Imagine you broke your leg in high school and never got it set right. What would happen? Would you ever walk again? Sure. Will it heal? Sure. Will it heal right? Probably not. You might have one leg shorter than the other, or progressive bone and joint problems. Time does heal all wounds, just not necessarily in the best way.

Some people may choose to take their chances and deal with the problem. The main reason for that is the fear of the solution. In order to fix the bone, it would need to be broken again and set properly. Voluntarily breaking a bone is not very appealing. On the other hand, neither is a lifetime of pain and problems walking. It would be even worse if someone had purposely broken your leg because every time you walked or had leg pain, you would be reminded of the person that hurt you. You would also be giving them power to extend that pain from the past to the present.

Even though time heals all wounds, there are better ways and worse ways to do that. Since you're reading this book, you are probably looking towards the better way. Dealing with trauma is very similar to dealing with the broken bone that was never dealt with. Confronting past pain can generate the same fears as re-breaking a bone or re-opening a wound. It is natural to avoid pain, but avoiding the pain won't help you walk any better. It's also temporary. The benefit gained confronting issues can be permanent.

It's too easy to say the past is the past and that I'm good now. It would also be great if that were true. For some, it is true. For many, not so much. So how do we know if we are "good"? One easy way to know is based on how willing and able we are to discuss the past. I was recently speaking with someone whose cousin had passed away. He was very distraught and in a dark place. He realized that and spoke with people in his support system and went to therapy for it. Naturally, it was difficult as he did not like talking about it, nor did he like the idea of "burdening" others. After several weeks, he reported that he was "okay". He missed his cousin, but was able to talk about it comfortably and focus on ways to celebrate his life instead of grieving his death.

Many people in similar situations avoid talking about it because it's painful. We often hold back tears and focus on other things to avoid that pain. When we do that, we often "shelve it". We haven't dealt with it, we just don't think about it. "Shelving" feelings has consequences. If we don't deal with our feelings, they will deal with us. Sadly, this can lead us to perpetuate the same issues we are dealing with and project them onto others. This is one of the main reasons that families have cycles of abuse.

How do we know if we are "okay"? One way to know is if we can talk about a past issue with insight. That insight often involves discussing what happened, what the impact was back then, and what the impact is now. The current impact can be in the form of insight into why we feel or do certain things. It can also be in the form of why we changed certain things over time. We'll go over some common diagnoses to see if we are being negatively controlled or influenced.

It's important to have context before looking at the concept of a diagnosis. Clinicians are trained to diagnose someone to see if they meet the criteria for an actual diagnosis. This is not to be confused with someone having symptoms or meeting some of the criteria for a diagnosis. In mental health, we use the Diagnostic and Statistical Manual of Mental Disorders–Fifth Edition (DSM-V) to assess patients. This section is meant to create some working knowledge to know if more information is needed. Similar to WebMD, it is not meant for the reader to diagnose. If there are indicators, it could certainly be helpful to speak with a professional.

Some disorders are organic in nature. They have little to do with environment and would happen regardless. Some disorders are more experience-based and can be understood through a psycho-social exploration. In other words, some are simply nature versus nurture. Many are a combination, but working on one can help with the other. For example, medication for depression has a physical effect on the brain and helps with the transmission of neurotransmitters to help someone feel less depressed. While on medication, a person can explore what experiences contributed to the depression, work on alternative ways to cope with the causes, and possibly reduce the need for medication.

Before exploring diagnoses, it's important to define adverse childhood experiences (ACEs) since often they contribute to mental health issues. According to the Center for Disease Control (CDC), Adverse childhood experiences, or ACEs, are potentially traumatic events that occur in childhood (0-17 years). For example:

- experiencing violence, abuse, or neglect
- witnessing violence in the home or community
- having a family member attempt or die by suicide

Also included are aspects of the child's environment that can undermine their sense of safety, stability, and bonding, such as growing up in a household with:

- substance use problems
- mental health problems
- instability due to parental separation or household members being in jail or prison

Please note that the examples above are not a complete list of adverse experiences. Many other traumatic experiences could impact health and wellbeing, such as not having enough food to eat, experiencing homelessness or unstable housing, or experiencing discrimination.

ACEs are linked to chronic health problems, mental illness, and substance use problems in adolescence and adulthood. ACEs can also negatively impact education, job opportunities, and earning potential. However, ACEs can be resolved The best window is usually early on. Through early detection and intervention, we can, hopefully, minimize the impact of the negative event. As we explore the different forms of impact, we can better recognize symptoms in others and pass our knowledge onto them.

When I took an abnormal psychology class, I identified with too many of the items in the criteria than I care to admit. Most people who take the class say the same thing, that we all identify with many symptoms of different diagnoses as we've experienced some of them from time to time. So remember, identifying with the symptoms does not mean you have the diagnosis.

Depression

We'll start with depression, since that's the first one in the DSM-V. According to the American Psychiatric Association, depression (major depressive disorder) is a common and serious medical illness that negatively affects how you feel, the way you think, and how you act. Fortunately, it is also treatable. Depression causes feelings of sadness and/or a loss of interest in activities you once enjoyed. It can lead to a variety of emotional and physical problems and can decrease your ability to function at work and at home.

Depression symptoms can vary from mild to severe and can include:

- Feeling sad or having a depressed mood
- Loss of interest or pleasure in activities once enjoyed
- Changes in appetite—weight loss or gain unrelated to dieting
- Trouble sleeping or sleeping too much
- Loss of energy or increased fatigue
- Increase in purposeless physical activity (e.g., inability to sit still, pacing, hand wringing) or slowed movements or speech (these actions must be severe enough to be observable by others)
- Feeling worthless or guilty
- Difficulty thinking, concentrating or making decisions
- Thoughts of death or suicide

Symptoms must last at least two weeks and must represent a change in your previous level of functioning for a diagnosis of depression. Also, medical conditions (e.g., thyroid problems, a brain tumor, or vitamin deficiency) can mimic symptoms of depression, so it is important to rule out general medical causes.

Depression affects an estimated one in 15 adults (6.7%) in any given year. And one in six people (16.6%) will experience depression at some time in their life. Depression can occur at any time, but on average, first appears during the late teens to mid-twenties. Women are more likely than men to experience depression. Some studies show that one-third of women will experience a major depressive episode in their lifetime. There is a high degree of heritability (approximately 40%) when first-degree relatives (parents/children/siblings) have depression. Heritability refers to genetic predisposition.

The death of a loved one, loss of a job, or the ending of a relationship are difficult experiences for a person to endure. It is normal for feelings of sadness or grief to develop in response to such situations. Those experiencing loss often describe themselves as being "depressed", but being sad is not the same as having depression. The grieving process is natural and unique to each individual and shares some of the same features of depression. Both grief and depression may involve intense sadness and withdrawal from usual activities. They are also different in important ways:

- In grief, painful feelings come in waves, often intermixed with positive memories of the deceased. In major depression, mood and/or interest (pleasure) are decreased for most of two weeks.
- In grief, self-esteem is usually maintained. In major depression, feelings of worthlessness and self-loathing are common.
- In grief, thoughts of death may surface when thinking of or fantasizing about "joining" the deceased loved one. In major depression, thoughts are focused on ending one's life due to feeling worthless or undeserving of living or being unable to cope with the pain of depression.

Grief and depression can co-exist. For some people, the death of a loved one, losing a job or being a victim of a physical assault or a major disaster can lead to depression. When grief and depression co-occur, the grief is more severe and lasts longer than grief without depression. Distinguishing between grief and depression is important and can assist people in getting the help, support or treatment they need.

Depression can affect anyone—even a person who appears to live in relatively ideal circumstances. Several factors can play a role in depression:

- Biochemistry: Differences in certain chemicals in the brain may contribute to symptoms of depression.
- Genetics: Depression can run in families. For example, if one identical twin has depression, the other has a 70 percent chance of having the illness sometime in life.
- Personality: People with low self-esteem, who are easily overwhelmed by stress, or who are generally pessimistic appear to be more likely to experience depression.
- Environmental factors: Continuous exposure to violence, neglect, abuse or poverty may make some people more vulnerable to depression.

Depression is among the most treatable of mental disorders. Between 80% and 90% percent of people with depression eventually respond well to treatment. Almost all patients gain some relief from their symptoms. Before a diagnosis or treatment, a health professional should conduct a thorough diagnostic evaluation, including an interview and a physical examination. In some cases, a blood test might be done to make sure the depression is not due to a medical condition like a thyroid problem or a vitamin deficiency (reversing the medical cause would alleviate the depression-like symptoms). The evaluation will identify specific symptoms and explore medical and family histories as well as cultural and environmental factors with the goal of arriving at a diagnosis and planning a course of action.

Medication

Brain chemistry may contribute to an individual's depression and may factor into their treatment. For this reason, antidepressants might be prescribed to help modify one's brain chemistry. These medications are not sedatives, "uppers" or tranquilizers. They are not habit-forming. Generally, antidepressant medications have no stimulating effect on people not experiencing depression.

Antidepressants may produce some improvement within the first week or two of use, yet full benefits may not be seen for two to three months. If a patient feels little or no improvement after several weeks, his or her psychiatrist can alter the dose of the medication or add or substitute another antidepressant. In some situations, other psychotropic medications may be helpful. It is important to let your doctor know if a medication does not work or if you experience side effects.

Psychiatrists usually recommend that patients continue to take medication for six or more months after the symptoms have improved. Longer-term maintenance treatment may be suggested to decrease the risk of future episodes for certain people at high risk.

Psychotherapy

Psychotherapy, or "talk therapy", is sometimes used alone for the treatment of mild depression; for moderate to severe depression, psychotherapy is often used along with antidepressant medications. Cognitive behavioral therapy (CBT) has been found to be effective in treating depression. CBT is a form of therapy focused on the problem-solving in the present. CBT helps a person to recognize distorted/negative thinking with the goal of changing thoughts and behaviors to respond to challenges in a more positive manner.

Psychotherapy may involve only the individual, but it can include others. For example, family or couples therapy can help address issues within these close relationships. Group therapy brings people with similar illnesses together in a supportive environment, and can assist the participant in learning how others cope in similar situations. Depending on the severity of the depression, treatment can take a few weeks or much longer. In many cases, significant improvement can be made in 10 to 15 sessions.

EMDR is a very popular treatment for helping cope with trauma. Eye Movement Desensitization and Reprocessing (EMDR) is a distinctive, evidence-based psychotherapy approach developed by Francine Shapiro in the late 1980s. It's designed to help people recover from trauma and other distressing life experiences, including PTSD, anxiety, depression, and panic disorders. The core premise of EMDR therapy is that many psychological difficulties are the result of distressing life experiences not fully processed at the time they occur, leading to maladaptive coping mechanisms.

How EMDR Works

EMDR therapy is structured into eight phases, focusing on the past, present, and future aspects of a traumatic or distressing event. The goal is to process these experiences fully, reducing their lingering effects and allowing for adaptive coping mechanisms to take their place. The process includes:

History and Treatment Planning: The therapist gathers information about the client's history and decides which targets need processing.

Preparation: The therapist explains the EMDR process and teaches stress reduction techniques for the client to use during and between sessions.

Assessment: Identifying the specific target for the session, including a vivid visual image related to the memory, a negative belief about the self, and related emotions and body sensations.

Desensitization: This involves focusing on the memory while engaging in EMDR processing using bilateral stimulation (typically eye movements), which is believed to facilitate the reprocessing of the memory.

Installation: The focus is on strengthening positive beliefs related to the target memory.

Body Scan: After the positive belief is strengthened, the client is asked to scan their body for any residual tension or unusual sensations, which are then targeted for reprocessing.

Closure: The session ends with the therapist guiding the client back to equilibrium, regardless of whether the reprocessing of the target memory was completed.

Reevaluation: At the beginning of the next session, the therapist checks the progress made and decides whether further reprocessing is needed.

The Role of Bilateral Stimulation

Bilateral stimulation is a hallmark of EMDR therapy, most commonly in the form of guided eye movements. The client is directed to move their eyes back and forth following the therapist's hand or another object. This is believed to mimic the psychological state associated with Rapid Eye Movement (REM) sleep, facilitating information processing. Other forms of bilateral stimulation can include auditory tones or tactile taps.

Effectiveness and Applications

Research has supported EMDR's effectiveness, particularly for PTSD, with many clients reporting a reduction in the vividness and emotional charge of their traumatic memories. It has also been found to be effective for a variety of other psychological issues.

Why It Might Work

The exact mechanisms by which EMDR works are still under investigation. One theory is that the bilateral stimulation used in EMDR helps with the accessing and processing of traumatic memories, making them less distressing. It may also reduce the vividness or emotional intensity of the memory, making it easier to manage.

EMDR is a complex therapeutic approach that requires special training for the therapists who provide it. It's considered a powerful tool for helping people move past trauma and other distressing experiences by allowing them to process these memories in a safe and controlled environment.

Anxiety

Anxiety is a normal reaction to stress. Mild levels of anxiety can be beneficial in some situations. It can alert us to dangers and help us prepare and pay attention. Anxiety disorders differ from normal feelings of nervousness or anxiousness and involve excessive fear or anxiety. Anxiety disorders are the most common of mental disorders. They affect nearly 30% of adults at some point in their lives. However, anxiety disorders are treatable with a number of psychotherapeutic treatments. Treatment helps most people lead normal, productive lives.

Anxiety refers to anticipation of a future concern and is more associated with muscle tension and avoidance behavior. Fear is an emotional response to an immediate threat and is more associated with a fight or flight reaction–either staying to fight or leaving to escape danger. Anxiety disorders can cause people to try to avoid situations that trigger or worsen their symptoms. Job performance, schoolwork, and personal relationships can be affected. In general, for a person to be diagnosed with an anxiety disorder, the fear or anxiety must:

- Be out of proportion to the situation or be age-inappropriate
- Hinder their ability to function normally

Generalized anxiety disorder involves persistent and excessive worry that interferes with daily activities. This ongoing worry and tension may be accompanied by physical symptoms, such as restlessness, feeling on edge or easily fatigued, difficulty concentrating, muscle tension, or problems sleeping. Often, the worries focus on everyday things such as job responsibilities, family health, or minor matters such as chores, car repairs, or appointments.

Panic disorder is recurrent panic attacks, an overwhelming combination of physical and psychological distress. During an attack, several of these symptoms occur in combination:

- Palpitations, pounding heart or rapid heart rate
- Sweating
- Trembling or shaking
- Feeling of shortness of breath or smothering sensations
- Chest pain
- Feeling dizzy, light-headed, or faint
- Feeling of choking
- Numbness or tingling
- Chills or hot flashes
- Nausea or abdominal pains
- Feeling detached
- Fear of losing control
- Fear of dying

Because the symptoms can be quite severe, some people who experience a panic attack may believe they are having a heart attack or some other life-threatening illness. They may go to a hospital emergency department. Panic attacks may be expected, such as a response to a feared object, or unexpected, apparently occurring for no reason. The mean age for onset of panic disorder is 20-24. Panic attacks may occur with other mental disorders such as depression or PTSD.

The causes of anxiety disorders are currently unknown but likely involve a combination of factors including genetic, environmental, psychological, and developmental. Anxiety disorders can run in families, suggesting that a combination of genes and environmental stresses can produce the disorders.

Diagnosis and Treatment

The first step is to see your doctor to make sure there is no physical problem causing the symptoms. If an anxiety disorder is diagnosed, a mental health professional can work with you on finding the best treatment. Unfortunately, many people with anxiety disorders don't seek help. They don't realize that they have a condition for which there are effective treatments.

Although each anxiety disorder has unique characteristics, most respond well to two types of treatment: psychotherapy and medications. These treatments can be given alone or in combination. Cognitive behavior therapy (CBT) can help a person learn a different way of thinking, reacting, and behaving to help feel less anxious. Medications will not cure anxiety disorders, but can provide significant relief from symptoms. The most commonly used medications are antianxiety medications (generally prescribed only for a short period of time) and antidepressants. Beta-blockers, used for heart conditions, are sometimes used to control physical symptoms of anxiety.

There are a number of things people do to help cope with symptoms of anxiety disorders and make treatment more effective. Stress management techniques and meditation can be helpful. Support groups (in-person or online) can provide an opportunity to share experiences and coping strategies. Learning more about the specifics of a disorder and helping family and friends to understand the condition better can also be helpful. Avoid caffeine, which can worsen symptoms, and check with your doctor about any medications.

Obsessive Compulsive Disorder (OCD)

Obsessive Compulsive Disorder can be caused by trauma and abuse in one's life. For many, it is due to an internal need to control one's environment due to feeling a lack of control in other areas. According to the APA, Obsessive Compulsive Disorder (OCD) is a disorder in which people have recurring, unwanted thoughts, ideas, or sensations (obsessions). To get rid of the thoughts, they feel driven to do something repetitively (compulsions). Repetitive behaviors, such as handwashing/cleaning, checking on things, and mental acts like (counting) or other activities, can significantly interfere with a person's daily activities and social interactions.

Many people without OCD have distressing thoughts or repetitive behaviors. However, these do not typically disrupt daily life. For people with OCD, thoughts are persistent and intrusive, and behaviors are rigid. Not performing the behaviors commonly causes great distress, often attached to a specific fear of dire consequences (to self or loved ones) if the behaviors are not completed. Many people with OCD know or suspect their obsessional thoughts are not realistic; others may think they could be true. Even if they know their intrusive thoughts are not realistic, people with OCD have difficulty disengaging from the obsessive thoughts or stopping the compulsive actions.

A diagnosis of OCD requires the presence of obsessional thoughts and/or compulsions that are time-consuming (more than one hour a day), cause significant distress, and impair work or social functioning. OCD affects 2-3% of people in the United States, and among adults, slightly more women than men are affected. OCD often begins in childhood, adolescence, or early adulthood. Some people may have some symptoms of OCD but not meet the full criteria for this disorder.

Obsessions are recurrent and persistent thoughts, impulses, or images that cause distressing emotions such as anxiety, fear, or disgust. Many people with OCD recognize that these are a product of their mind and that they are excessive or unreasonable. However, the distress caused by these intrusive thoughts cannot be resolved by logic or reasoning. Most people with OCD try to ease the distress of the obsessional thinking, or undo the perceived threats, by using compulsions. They may also try to ignore or suppress the obsessions or distract themselves with other activities.

Examples of common content of obsessional thoughts are:

- Fear of contamination by people or the environment
- Disturbing sexual thoughts or images

- Religious, often blasphemous, thoughts or fears
- Fear of perpetrating aggression or being harmed (self or loved ones)
- Extreme worry something is not complete
- Extreme concern with order, symmetry, or precision
- Fear of losing or discarding something important
- Can also be seemingly meaningless thoughts, images, sounds, words or music

Compulsions are repetitive behaviors or mental acts that a person feels driven to perform in response to an obsession. The behaviors typically prevent or reduce a person's distress related to an obsession temporarily, and they are then more likely to do the same in the future. Compulsions may be excessive responses that are directly related to an obsession (such as excessive handwashing due to the fear of contamination) or actions that are completely unrelated to the obsession. In the most severe cases, a constant repetition of rituals may fill the day, making a normal routine impossible.

Examples of compulsions include:

- Excessive or ritualized handwashing, showering, brushing teeth, or toileting
- Repeated cleaning of household objects
- Ordering or arranging things in a particular way
- Repeatedly checking locks, switches, appliances, doors, etc.
- Constantly seeking approval or reassurance
- Rituals related to numbers, such as counting, repeating, excessively preferencing or avoiding certain numbers
- People with OCD may also avoid certain people, places, or situations that cause them distress and trigger obsessions and/ or compulsions. Avoiding these things may further impair their ability to function in life and may be detrimental to other areas of mental or physical health.

People with OCD who receive appropriate treatment commonly experience increased quality of life and improved functioning. Treatment may improve an individual's ability to function at school and work, develop and enjoy relationships, and pursue leisure activities.

One effective treatment is a type of cCBT known as exposure and response prevention (ERP). During treatment sessions, patients are exposed to feared situations or images that focus on their obsessions. Although it is standard to start with those that only lead to mild or moderate symptoms, initially, the treatment often causes increased anxiety.

Patients are instructed to avoid performing their usual compulsive behaviors (known as response prevention). By staying in a feared situation without anything terrible happening, patients learn that their fearful thoughts are just thoughts. People learn that they can cope with their thoughts without relying on ritualistic behaviors, and their anxiety decreases over time.

Using evidence-based guidelines, therapists and patients typically collaborate to develop an exposure plan that gradually moves from lower anxiety situations to higher anxiety situations. Exposures are performed both in treatment sessions and at home. Some people with OCD may not agree to participate in CBT because of the initial anxiety it evokes, but it is the most powerful tool available for treating many types of OCD.

A class of medications known as selective serotonin reuptake inhibitors (SSRIs), typically used to treat depression, can also be effective in the treatment of OCD. The SSRI dosage used to treat OCD is often higher than that used to treat depression. Patients who do not respond to one SSRI medication sometimes respond to another. The maximum benefit usually takes six to twelve weeks or longer to be fully visible. Patients with mild to moderate OCD symptoms are typically treated with either CBT or medication depending on patient preference, the patient's cognitive abilities and level of insight, the presence or absence of associated psychiatric conditions, and treatment availability. The best treatment of OCD is a combination of CBT and SSRIs, especially if OCD symptoms are severe. Other types of OCD include: body dysmorphic disorder, trichotillomania (Hair-Pulling Disorder), and excoriation (skin-picking disorder).

Post-Traumatic Stress Disorder

Post-traumatic stress disorder (PTSD) is a psychiatric disorder that may occur in people who have experienced or witnessed a traumatic event, series of events, or set of circumstances. An individual may experience this as emotionally or physically harmful or life-threatening and it may affect mental, physical, social, and/or spiritual well-being. Examples include natural disasters, serious accidents, terrorist acts, war/combat, rape/sexual assault, historical trauma, intimate partner violence and bullying,

PTSD has been known by many names in the past, such as "shell shock" during the years of World War I and "combat fatigue" after World War II, but PTSD does not just happen to combat veterans. PTSD can occur in all people, of any ethnicity, nationality or culture, and at any age. PTSD affects approximately 3.5 percent of U.S. adults every year. The lifetime prevalence of PTSD in adolescents ages 13–18 is 8%. An estimate one in 11 people will be diagnosed with PTSD in their lifetime. Women are twice as likely as men to have PTSD. Three ethnic groups–U.S. Latinos, African Americans, and Native Americans/Alaska Natives–are disproportionately affected and have higher rates of PTSD than non-Latino whites.

People with PTSD have intense, disturbing thoughts and feelings related to their experience that last long after the traumatic event has ended. They may relive the event through flashbacks or nightmares; they may feel sadness, fear or anger; and they may feel detached or estranged from other people. People with PTSD may avoid situations or people that remind them of the traumatic event, and they may have strong negative reactions to something as ordinary as a loud noise or an accidental touch.

A diagnosis of PTSD requires exposure to an upsetting traumatic event. Exposure includes directly experiencing an event, witnessing a traumatic event happening to others, or learning that a traumatic event happened to a close family member or friend. It can also occur as a result of repeated exposure to horrible details of trauma, such as police officers exposed to details of child abuse cases.

Symptoms of PTSD fall into the following four categories. Specific symptoms can vary in severity.

1. **Intrusion:** Intrusive thoughts such as repeated, involuntary memories, distressing dreams, or flashbacks of the traumatic event. Flashbacks may be so vivid that people feel they are reliving the traumatic experience or seeing it before their eyes.

2. **Avoidance:** Avoiding reminders of the traumatic event may include avoiding people, places, activities, objects and situations that may trigger distressing memories. People may try to avoid remembering or thinking about the traumatic event. They may resist talking about what happened or how they feel about it.

3. **Alterations in cognition and mood:** Inability to remember important aspects of the traumatic event, negative thoughts and feelings leading to ongoing and distorted beliefs about oneself or others (e.g., "I am bad," "No one can be trusted"); distorted thoughts about the cause or consequences of the event leading to wrongly blaming self or other; ongoing fear, horror, anger, guilt or shame; much less interest in activities previously enjoyed; feeling detached or estranged from others; or being unable to experience positive emotions (a void of happiness or satisfaction).

4. **Alterations in arousal and reactivity:** Arousal and reactive symptoms may include being irritable and having angry outbursts; behaving recklessly or in a self-destructive way; being overly watchful of one's surroundings in a suspecting way; being easily startled; or having problems concentrating or sleeping.

Many people who are exposed to a traumatic event experience symptoms similar to those described above in the days following the event. For a person to be diagnosed with PTSD, however, symptoms must last for more than a month and must cause significant distress or problems in the individual's daily functioning. Many individuals develop symptoms within three months of the trauma, but symptoms may appear later and often persist for months and sometimes years. PTSD often occurs with other related conditions, such as depression, substance use, memory problems, and other physical and mental health problems.

There are four conditions related to PTSD: acute stress disorder, adjustment disorder, disinhibited social engagement disorder, and reactive attachment disorder.

Acute stress disorder occurs in reaction to a traumatic event, just as PTSD does, and the symptoms are similar. However, the symptoms occur between three days and one month after the event. People with acute stress disorder may relive the trauma, have flashbacks or nightmares, and may feel numb or detached from themselves. These symptoms cause major distress and problems in their daily lives. About half of people with acute stress disorder go on to have PTSD. Acute stress disorder has been diagnosed in 19%–50% of individuals that experience interpersonal violence (e.g., rape, assault, intimate partner violence).

Psychotherapy, including CBT, can help control and prevent symptoms from getting worse and developing into PTSD. Medication, such as SSRI antidepressants, can help ease the symptoms.

Adjustment disorder occurs in response to a stressful life event (or events). The emotional or behavioral symptoms a person experiences in response to the stressor are generally more severe or more intense than what would be reasonably expected for the type of event that occurred.

Symptoms can include feeling tense, sad or hopeless; withdrawing from other people; acting defiantly or showing impulsive behavior; or physical manifestations like tremors, palpitations, and headaches. The symptoms cause significant distress or problems functioning in key areas of someone's life, for example, at work, school, or in social interactions. Symptoms of adjustment disorders begin within three months of a stressful event and last no longer than six months after the stressor or its consequences have ended.

The stressor may be a single event (such as a romantic breakup), or there may be more than one event with a cumulative effect. Stressors may be recurring or continuous (such as an ongoing painful illness with increasing disability). Stressors may affect a single individual, an entire family, or a larger group or community (for example, in the case of a natural disaster).

An estimated 5% to 20% of individuals in outpatient mental health treatment have a principal diagnosis of adjustment disorder. A recent study found that more than 15% of adults with cancer had adjustment disorder. It is typically treated with psychotherapy.

Disinhibited social engagement disorder occurs in children who have experienced severe social neglect or deprivation before the age of two. Similar to reactive attachment disorder, it can occur when children lack the basic emotional needs for comfort, stimulation, and affection, or when repeated changes in caregivers (such as frequent foster care changes) prevent them from forming stable attachments.

Disinhibited social engagement disorder involves a child engaging in overly familiar or culturally inappropriate behavior with unfamiliar adults. For example, the child may be willing to go off with an unfamiliar adult with minimal or no hesitation. Developmental delays including cognitive and language delays often co-occur with this disorder. Caregiving quality has been shown to mediate the course of this illness. Yet even with improvements in the caregiving environment, some children may have symptoms that persist through adolescence.

The prevalence of disinhibited social engagement disorder is unknown, but it is thought to be rare. Most severely neglected children do not develop the disorder. The most important treatment modality is to work with caregivers to ensure the child has an emotionally available attachment figure.

Reactive attachment disorder occurs in children who have experienced severe social neglect or deprivation during their first years of life. It can occur when children lack the basic emotional needs for comfort, stimulation and affection, or when repeated changes in caregivers (such as frequent foster care changes) prevent them from forming stable attachments.

Children with reactive attachment disorder are emotionally withdrawn from their adult caregivers. They rarely turn to caregivers for comfort, support or protection, or do not respond to comforting when they are distressed. During routine interactions with caregivers, they show little positive emotion and may show unexplained fear or sadness.

The problems appear before age 5. Developmental delays, especially cognitive and language delays, often occur along with the disorder.

Reactive attachment disorder is uncommon, even in severely neglected children. Treatment involves a therapist working with a child and their family to strengthen the relationship between the child and their primary caregivers.

It is important to note that not everyone who experiences trauma develops PTSD, and not everyone who develops PTSD requires psychiatric treatment. For some people, symptoms of PTSD subside or disappear over time. Others get better with the help of their support system (family, friends, or clergy). But many people with PTSD need professional treatment to recover from psychological distress that can be intense and disabling. It is important to remember that trauma may lead to severe distress. That distress is not the individual's fault, and PTSD is treatable. The earlier a person gets treatment, the better chance of recovery.

Psychiatrists and other mental health professionals use various effective (research-proven) methods to help people recover from PTSD. Both talk therapy (psychotherapy) and medication provide effective evidence-based treatments for PTSD.

One category of psychotherapy, cognitive behavior therapies (CBT), is very effective. Cognitive processing therapy, prolonged exposure therapy and stress inoculation therapy (described below) are among the types of CBT used to treat PTSD.

- Cognitive Processing Therapy is an evidence-based, cognitive behavioral therapy designed specifically to treat PTSD and comorbid symptoms. It focuses on changing painful negative emotions (such as shame, guilt, etc.) and beliefs (such as "I have failed;" "the world is dangerous") due to the trauma. Therapists help the person confront such distressing memories and emotions.
- Prolonged Exposure Therapy uses repeated, detailed imagining of the trauma or progressive exposures to symptom "triggers"

in a safe, controlled environment to help a person face and gain control of fear and distress and learn to cope. For example, virtual reality programs have been used to help war veterans with PTSD re-experience the battlefield in a controlled, therapeutic way.

- Trauma Focused Cognitive Behavioral Therapy is an evidence-based treatment model for children and adolescents that incorporates trauma-sensitive interventions with cognitive behavioral, family, and humanistic principles and techniques.

- Eye Movement Desensitization and Reprocessing for PTSD is a trauma-focused psychotherapy which is administered over approximately 3 months. This therapy helps a person to reprocess the memory of the trauma so that it is experienced in a different way. After a thorough history is taken and a treatment plan developed, the therapist guides the patient through questions about the traumatic memory. Eye movements similar to those in REM sleep are recreated during a session by having the patient watch the therapist's fingers go back and forth or by watching a light bar. The eye movements last for a brief time period and then stop. Experiences during a session may include changes in thoughts, images, and feelings. After repeated sessions, the memory tends to change and is experienced in a less negative manner.

- Group therapy encourages survivors of similar traumatic events to share their experiences and reactions in a comfortable and non-judgmental setting. Group members help one another realize that many people would have responded the same way and felt the same emotions. Family therapy may also help because the behavior and distress of the person with PTSD can affect the entire family.

Other psychotherapies, such as interpersonal, supportive and psychodynamic therapies, focus on the emotional and interpersonal aspects of PTSD. These may be helpful for people who do not want to expose themselves to reminders of their traumas.

Medication can help to control the symptoms of PTSD. In addition, the symptom relief that medication provides allows many people to participate more effectively in psychotherapy.

Some antidepressants, such as SSRIs and SNRIs (selective serotonin re-uptake inhibitors and serotonin-norepinephrine re-uptake inhibitors), are commonly used to treat the core symptoms of PTSD. They are used either alone or in combination with psychotherapy or other treatments.

Other medications may be used to lower anxiety and physical agitation, or treat the nightmares and sleep problems that trouble many people with PTSD.

Dissociative Disorders

According to the American Psychiatric Association, dissociative disorders involve problems with memory, identity, emotion, perception, behavior and sense of self. Dissociative symptoms can potentially disrupt every area of mental functioning.

Examples of dissociative symptoms include the experience of detachment or feeling as if one is outside one's body, and loss of memory or amnesia. Dissociative disorders are frequently associated with previous experience of trauma.

There are three types of dissociative disorders:

- Dissociative identity disorder
- Dissociative amnesia
- Depersonalization/derealization disorder

The Sidran Institute, which works to help people understand and cope with traumatic stress and dissociative disorders, describes the phenomenon of dissociation and the purpose it may serve as follows:

> Dissociation is a disconnection between a person's thoughts, memories, feelings, actions, or sense of who he or she is. This is a normal process that everyone has experienced. Examples of mild, common dissociation

include daydreaming, highway hypnosis, or "getting lost" in a book or movie, all of which involve "losing touch" with awareness of one's immediate surroundings.

During a traumatic experience such as an accident, disaster, or crime victimization, dissociation can help a person tolerate what might otherwise be too difficult to bear. In situations like these, a person may dissociate the memory of the place, circumstances, or feelings about the overwhelming event, mentally escaping from the fear, pain, and horror. This may make it difficult to later remember the details of the experience, as reported by many disaster and accident survivors.

Dissociative Identity Disorder

Dissociative identity disorder is associated with overwhelming experiences, traumatic events, and/or abuse that occurred in childhood. Dissociative identity disorder was previously referred to as multiple personality disorder.

Symptoms of dissociative identity disorder (criteria for diagnosis) include:

- The existence of two or more distinct identities (or "personality states"). The distinct identities are accompanied by changes in behavior, memory, and thinking. The signs and symptoms may be observed by others or reported by the individual.
- Ongoing gaps in memory about everyday events, personal information, and/or past traumatic events.
- The symptoms cause significant distress or problems in social, occupational, or other areas of functioning.

In addition, the disturbance must not be a normal part of a broadly accepted cultural or religious practice. In many cultures around the world, experiences of being possessed are a normal part of spiritual practice and are not dissociative disorders.

The attitude and personal preferences (for example, about food, activities, clothes) of a person with dissociative identity disorder may suddenly shift and then shift back. The shifts in identities happen involuntarily, are unwanted, and cause distress. People with dissociative identity disorder may feel that they have suddenly become observers of their own speech and actions, or their bodies may feel different (e.g., like a small child, like the opposite gender, huge and muscular).

The Sidran Institute notes that a person with dissociative identity disorder "feels as if she has within her two or more entities, each with its own way of thinking and remembering about herself and her life. It is important to keep in mind that although these alternate states may feel or appear to be very different, they are all manifestations of a single, whole person." Other names used to describe these alternate states including "alternate personalities", "alters", "states of consciousness", and "identities."

For people with dissociative identity disorder, the extent of problems in functioning can vary widely, from minimal to significant problems. People often try to minimize the impact of their symptoms.

People who have experienced physical and sexual abuse in childhood are at increased risk of dissociative identity disorder. The vast majority of people who develop dissociative disorders have experienced repetitive, overwhelming trauma in childhood. Among people with dissociative identity disorder in the United States, Canada and Europe, about 90 percent have been the victims of childhood abuse and neglect.

Suicide attempts and other self-injurious behavior are common among people with dissociative identity disorder. More than 70 percent of outpatients with dissociative identity disorder have attempted suicide. With appropriate treatment, many people are successful in addressing the major symptoms of dissociative identity disorder and improving their ability to function and live a productive, fulfilling life.

Treatment typically involves psychotherapy. Therapy can help people gain control over the dissociative process and symptoms. The goal of therapy is to help integrate the different elements of identity. Therapy may be intense and difficult as it involves remembering and coping with past traumatic experiences. Cognitive behavioral therapy and dialectical behavioral therapy are two commonly used types of therapy. Hypnosis has also been found to be helpful in the treatment of dissociative identity disorder.

There are no medications to directly treat the symptoms of dissociative identity disorder. However, medication may be helpful in treating related conditions or symptoms, such as using antidepressants to treat symptoms of depression.

Depersonalization/Derealization Disorder

Depersonalization/derealization disorder involves significant ongoing or recurring experience of one or both conditions:

- Depersonalization – experiences of unreality or detachment from one's mind, self or body. People may feel like they are outside their bodies and watching events happening to them.
- Derealization – experiences of unreality or detachment from one's surroundings. People may feel things and people in the world around them are not real.

During these altered experiences, the person is aware of reality and that their experience is unusual. The experience can be very distressing, even though the person may appear to be unreactive or lacking emotion. Symptoms may begin in early childhood; the average age a person first experiences the disorder is 16. Less than 20 percent of people with depersonalization/derealization disorder first experience symptoms after age 20.

Dissociative Amnesia

Dissociative amnesia involves not being able to recall information about oneself, such as their name or address. This amnesia is usually related to a traumatic or stressful event and may be:

- localized – the person is unable to remember an event or period of time (most common type)

- selective – the person is unable to remember a specific aspect of an event or some events within a period of time
- generalized – the person experiences a complete loss of identity and life history (rare)

Dissociative amnesia is associated with having experiences of childhood trauma, and particularly with experiences of emotional abuse and emotional neglect. People may not be aware of their memory loss or may have only limited awareness. They may also minimize the importance of memory loss about a particular event or time.

Conclusion

This is not meant to be an all-inclusive list, but it should give you a good sense of how various psychological diagnoses can be influenced by negative life experiences. As you read through it, there were likely pieces that caused you to reflect on yourself. There were also probably pieces that stood out for you as you considered other people in your life. As mentioned before, the chapter is only meant to highlight possible red flags or signs.

Red flags are areas that require attention rather than just ignoring. Some of the issues may even be past tense for you, and you may have done the work already. If that's the case, you're already familiar with the information and have applied it to be more in control of your life. Keep reading to see what else you can learn or reflect on.

Chapter 3

WHAT IS POWER?

God, grant me the serenity
to accept the things I cannot change,
the courage to change the things I can,
and the wisdom to know the difference.
– Reinhold Niebuhr

The serenity prayer is familiar to many people. It is the mantra at many Alcoholics Anonymous meetings. It is also one of the most powerful concepts to incorporate into our lives. It actually speaks to power on many levels. It speaks to submission to a higher power, which is meaningful and impactful to many people. It also speaks to our own power as well as the power we give unto others. These latter two aspects of power is what we'll be speaking about in this chapter.

I've always been fascinated with the concept of power. The power I'm referring to is our own power as it pertains to ourself. It's an internal construct about what power we have and what power we allow other entities have over us. It's largely based on how we think and how we choose to think. It's one of the few things we actually have control over, and when we master it, it gives us control over most things in our lives. When we really own this concept, we have a lot more control over our feelings and our behaviors. It's one of the easiest concepts that, when it clicks for us, makes our lives dramatically easier and happier.

Controlling Thoughts

Controlling one's thoughts can be challenging, but there are strategies that can help you manage and direct your thinking. Here are some tips:

Mindfulness Meditation: Practice mindfulness to become aware of your thoughts without judgment. Meditation can help you observe your thoughts and let them pass without getting entangled in them.

Positive Affirmations: Replace negative thoughts with positive affirmations. Repeat positive statements to yourself to shift your mindset and focus on more constructive thinking.

Cognitive Behavioral Therapy (CBT): CBT techniques involve identifying and challenging negative thought patterns. By recognizing and changing irrational thoughts, you can positively impact your emotions and behaviors.

Set Goals and Prioritize: Establish clear goals and priorities. When your mind starts wandering to unproductive thoughts, redirect it by focusing on your goals and what you need to accomplish.

Create a Thought Journal: Keep a journal to record your thoughts. This can help you identify patterns, triggers, and areas where you may need to change your thinking.

Practice Gratitude: Regularly reflect on things you're grateful for. Shifting your focus to positive aspects of your life can help counteract negative thoughts.

Limit Negative Influences: Be mindful of the media, people, or environments that contribute to negative thinking. Limit exposure to negativity and surround yourself with positive influences.

Exercise and Healthy Lifestyle: Regular physical activity can have positive effects on your mental well-being. A healthy lifestyle, including proper sleep and nutrition, can also contribute to better thought control.

Seek Professional Help: If you find it challenging to control your thoughts, consider seeking help from a mental health professional. They can provide guidance and support tailored to your specific situation. Remember, learning how to control your thoughts is a gradual process, and it's okay to seek assistance when needed.

Think and be happy

The phrase **"think and be happy"** emphasizes the connection between our thoughts and our emotional state. While it may sound simplistic, there is truth to the idea that our thoughts play a significant role in shaping our emotions and overall well-being. Here are a few strategies to cultivate a more positive mindset:

Practice Gratitude: Regularly reflect on the things you're grateful for. This can shift your focus from what's lacking to what you appreciate in your life. This concept is very cool because it's something everyone has done at some point. We've all had times when we were feeling down before seeing someone who is suffering a hardship that makes us realize our situation is not so bad. Our happiness should not be based on someone else's possible sadness, but those moments help us seeour situation from a different perspective. When we tap into that process, we can do it deliberately rather than instinctively.

Positive Affirmations: Use positive affirmations to challenge and overcome self-sabotaging and negative thoughts. Repeat uplifting statements to yourself to foster a more positive mindset. We are all flawed and there is peace in accepting that. It makes us more tolerant of other people's flaws and less likely to condemn ourselves as harshly for our own shortcomings.

Focus on the Present: Engage in mindfulness by focusing on the present moment. When your mind starts dwelling on the past or worrying about the future, bring your attention back to the here and now. It's especially important not to "snowball" your problems by thinking about all of them at once. There's an exercise below that helps you with this.

Surround Yourself with Positivity: Spend time with positive and supportive people. Surrounding yourself with a positive social environment can have a significant impact on your own mindset. Remember, we attract what we put out. We have a better chance of being around positive people when we are positive. If you have a lot of negative people around you, it may be time to reflect on why that is.

Engage in Activities You Enjoy: Make time for activities that bring you joy and fulfillment. Engaging in hobbies and interests can contribute to a more positive outlook. It's okay to have a "healthy selfishness" where you engage in activities that make you feel good. It's a way to refresh ourselves and may also be a way to positively cope. Working out six days a week is my way of taking care of myself. I have never missed a week and don't plan on doing so. I'm flexible on when I go, but rigid about making sure I do. What activities do you do? If the answer is none, start thinking about which ones you'd like to do.

Practice Self-Compassion: Treat yourself with kindness and understanding. Don't be too harsh on yourself when facing challenges or setbacks. The only failures are the ones you don't learn from. Make a point to learn and grow from each setback.

Limit Negative Influences: Be mindful of the media, conversations, or environments that contribute to negativity. Limit exposure to sources that bring you down. Research shows us that people who spend more time on social media have higher rates of depression, and people who spend more time watching news have higher levels of anxiety.

Set Realistic Goals: Break down larger goals into smaller, achievable steps. Celebrate your successes, no matter how small, and acknowledge your progress.

Cultivate a Positive Mindset: Train yourself to notice and challenge negative thoughts. Instead of dwelling on what could go wrong, focus on what could go right. This is a powerful habit to develop. One of my personal goals is to maintain positive thinking. When I start thinking negatively about something or someone, I look in the mirror and say, "What are you doing?" After that, I change how I look at whatever caused it. If I can't change it, I choose not to focus on it. How we feed our thoughts is how we feed our emotions. From a logical point of view, why would we ever feed it negativity?

Laugh and Find Humor: Incorporate laughter into your life. Whether through comedy, spending time with funny friends, or finding humor in everyday situations, laughter can be a powerful mood booster. On a deeper level, there is much to be said about the mind-body connection and the power of laughter. There are reported cases of people with terminal illnesses that have extended their projected lifespan by watching comedy shows and movies.

It's important to note that being happy is not about denying or suppressing negative emotions but developing a balanced and positive perspective. Cultivating a positive mindset is a gradual process that involves conscious effort and practice.

Exercise Time!

We're going to try an exercise that will help you explore where your power lies and cut out half of your stress at the same time. I use this exercise with patients and it can have remarkable results. It's also really easy. Take a sheet of paper and make three columns. It may be easier to have the paper sideways (landscape). In the first column, list all the problems and stressors you have in your life. In the second column, list the items from the first column that you actually have control over.

Things we have control over
While we can't control every aspect of our lives, there are several things that individuals typically have some degree of control over. Here are some examples:

Attitude and Perspective: We have control over our attitude and how we choose to perceive and respond to situations.

Actions and Behavior: We can control our actions and behavior, including the choices we make and how we respond to challenges.

Personal Habits: Choices related to health, time management, and personal development fall within our control.

Communication: We have control over how we communicate with others, including the tone we use, the words we choose, and our listening skills.

Reactions to Situations: While we may not control external events, we can control how we react to them. This involves managing emotions and choosing constructive responses.

Learning and Growth: We have control over our commitment to learning and personal growth. This includes acquiring new skills, seeking knowledge, and adapting to change.

Relationships: While we can't control others, we have control over our actions within relationships, setting boundaries, and choosing whom we surround ourselves with.

Self-Care: Prioritizing self-care activities, such as exercise, adequate sleep, and relaxation, is within our control.

Setting Goals: We can set and work towards personal and professional goals, taking steps to achieve them over time.

Time Management: How we allocate our time and prioritize tasks is within our control. Effective time management can contribute to productivity and reduced stress.

It's important to recognize the balance between what we can control and what is beyond our control. Accepting the things we cannot change and focusing on the aspects we can influence can contribute to a healthier and more empowered mindset. With this in mind, complete column two with items you have control over.

Things we have no control over

While there are many aspects of our lives that we can control, there are also numerous factors beyond our control. This will be column three. Take the items from column one that you don't have control over and put them here. Some examples of what we don't have control over are:

Other People's Actions: We cannot control how other people behave, think, or make decisions. We can influence them to some extent, but we cannot dictate their actions.

Natural Events: Natural disasters, weather conditions, and other natural events are beyond our control. While we can take precautions, we cannot prevent or control these occurrences.

Others' Opinions and Perceptions: People will form their own opinions and perceptions of us, and we cannot control or dictate how others view or judge us.

Past Events: The past is beyond our control. While we can learn from it, we cannot change what has already happened.

Global and Economic Factors: Large-scale economic trends, global political events, and other macro-level factors are often beyond an individual's control.

Death and Aging: The inevitability of death and the natural aging process are aspects of life that we cannot control.

Genetic Factors: Our genetic makeup, inherited traits, and predispositions are largely beyond our control.

Random Events: Some events in life are purely random and unpredictable, such as accidents or unexpected changes.

Others' Feelings: We cannot control how others feel, and people's emotions are influenced by a variety of factors beyond our control.

Certain Health Conditions: While we can take steps to maintain good health, some health conditions and genetic predispositions may be beyond our control.

Understanding and accepting the limitations of control can contribute to a more resilient and adaptive mindset. It's essential to focus on managing and influencing what we can while acknowledging and adapting to the realities of what is beyond our control. To bring this point home, I want you to tear off column three, rip it up and throw it out. I'd say burn it, but as a fireman, that wouldn't be good. By destroying it, you're conceding you don't have control over these problems or stressors. If you don't have control over it, there is no purpose to giving it an energy or emotion. When this sinks in, you will literally cut your stress in half.

Prioritizing problems

So, what do you do with column two? Get to work. The most systematic way is to number them in order of priority. Prioritizing problems is a crucial skill for effective problem-solving and decision-making. Here's a step-by-step guide on how to prioritize problems:

Understand the Urgency: Assess the urgency of each problem. Some issues may require immediate attention, while others can be addressed over a more extended period.

Evaluate the Impact: Consider the potential impact of each problem. Some issues may have more significant consequences or affect multiple areas of your life, making them higher priorities.

Determine Feasibility: Evaluate the feasibility of solving each problem. Some issues may have straightforward solutions, while others may require more time, resources, or external assistance.

Consider Dependencies: Identify any dependencies between problems. Some issues may need to be addressed before others can be effectively resolved.

Align with Goals and Values: Consider how each problem aligns with your long-term goals and values. Prioritize problems that have a more significant impact on your overall well-being and objectives.

Assess Emotional Impact: Take into account the emotional toll of each problem. Addressing issues that have a significant emotional impact on your well-being can lead to a more balanced and resilient life.

Use a Prioritization Matrix: Create a prioritization matrix where you can assign scores to each problem based on factors like urgency, impact, feasibility, and alignment with goals. This can help you objectively assess and compare different issues.

Consider Time Sensitivity: Some problems may become more challenging to solve if left unaddressed. Consider the time sensitivity of each problem and whether delaying a resolution could lead to more significant challenges.

Seek Input from Others: If you're dealing with complex issues, consider seeking input from trusted colleagues, friends, or mentors. They may offer valuable perspectives that can influence your prioritization.

Create an Action Plan: Once you've prioritized the problems, create a detailed action plan for addressing them. Break down the steps needed to solve each problem and allocate resources accordingly.

Remember that prioritization is a dynamic process, and your priorities may shift as circumstances change. Regularly reassess and adjust your priorities based on evolving situations and new information. The most important thing is to tackle one problem at a time. If you're everywhere, then you're nowhere. It's why we get overwhelmed. We either get spread too thin and feel ineffective, or we get discouraged from the "snowballing" and don't even try.

The important part is to focus on one at a time. As you do that, you will whittle away at your list. As you do that, your list gets smaller and your areas of stress decrease. Let's start with a common one: improve a relationship. One of the main stressors we often have involves strained relationships. This can be with a family member, a partner, a friend, etc. This item usually falls into both lists because we can't control others. We do, however, have an impact on how others interact with us based on how we interact with them.

Improving relationships

Relationship problems can be one of the most disempowering struggles, as it's very easy to see what the other person does "wrong" and we can clearly see what we do "right". That lens leaves very little room for growth or improvement. There is great power in realizing what we do "wrong". The concept of right and wrong is very subjective and may be better contextualized as helpful or not helpful.

One way to have a more balanced view is to look at the situation from the other person's perspective. What are their intentions when they do things that aren't productive? What's their view of us? If it's bad, why? Questions can lead to more questions, but they can also lead to dialogue. We also have the power to choose how we see the other person. If we choose to see them negatively, we will focus on that negativity. The opposite is also true.

The power to improve relationships lies in the actions, attitudes, and behaviors of individuals within the relationship. Here are some ways individuals can empower themselves to enhance and strengthen their relationships:

Effective Communication: Develop strong communication skills. Actively listen to your partner, express your thoughts and feelings clearly, and work on understanding each other's perspectives. When Christine and I were dating, we had a handwritten sign on the refrigerator that read, "Effective communication is speaking without offending and listening without defending." Two simple statements that involve a lot of thought and effort.

To speak without offending means that you have to think about the words you want to say before you say them. The point of speaking is to be heard. We all hear differently, so to be effectively heard, we have to consider how the other person will best hear what we are trying to communicate.

To listen without defending means you have to try to hear and understand what is being said while resisting our tendencies to concurrently formulate a defense for what is being said. This is, arguably, more difficult. To be really good at it, we must reduce our emotional experience and tap into what the person is trying to communicate. It basically means that you have to ask yourself, "What are they trying to say to me?" It can be really tough to decipher what someone else is saying. It's even tougher when the person is speaking from emotion, which can include yelling and unpleasant language.

When my wife and I were dating, we devised our "rules of engagement". These rules keep us from using negative behaviors that would instantly derail any chance of hearing each other. Those rules are: no yelling, cursing, sarcasm, or bringing up family. Yes, they are still rules for us, although they have been broken from time to time. They are good rules to use in any relationship, not just with our partners. We'll discuss them more in a later chapter, as well as a number of other communication tools.

Empathy: Cultivate empathy by putting yourself in your partner's shoes. Understanding and acknowledging their emotions and experiences can foster a deeper connection. This is very difficult, especially if we feel we are not being heard. In *Seven Habits of Highly Effective People*, one of the habits is "seek to understand, then be understood." When we are able to actually show understanding, it increases the chances that the other person will try to understand as well.

We often try to show understanding by saying we understand, but that doesn't actually say much. It's better to repeat the concept being conveyed using different words to establish an understanding. If we're right, they will often speak more and also seek to understand us better. If we're wrong, they'll correct us and say it differently. This still shows an attempt and keeps the conversation moving.

It's important to note that empathy is different from sympathy. Empathy means understanding someone's emotions or experience, which enables us to identify what they need in order to support them. Sympathy means to take on the emotion of the other person. In some ways, that can feel good to people, but in actuality, you now have two people feeling the same emotion, which can effective decision-making. The worst-case scenario is this can lead to negative coping skills and make the situation worse.

Self-Awareness: Be aware of your own emotions, triggers, and communication style. Understanding yourself better can contribute to more effective and considerate interactions with your partner. It's easy to regard our own behaviors as just part of who we are, but that's really a cop out. The reality is, we are who we choose to be. There's a big difference in those two statements.

Attributing our behaviors as just part of who we are is an excuse for us to behave in a way that is often contrary to who we want to be. It's also disempowering to chalk our actions off as who we are is if we are stuck as that person. As we go through this book, we will see just how stifling and limiting that thought process can be. When we are self-aware, we can see how we may be handling a situation poorly based on our emotions and experiences. We can also choose to speak and behave differently once we do the work.

Conflict Resolution Skills: Learn and practice healthy conflict resolution skills. Instead of avoiding conflicts, address them constructively, focusing on finding solutions rather than placing blame. People often confuse conflict as a right and wrong. As a result, we battle to prove we are right and the other person is wrong. Disagreeing does not have to mean wrong and right. It just means both people have a different viewpoint or opinion on the issue being discussed. When we look to be right, we create an unwinnable situation as we are looking to force the other person to see that they are wrong.

In conflict resolution, it is far more effective to look for a win-win solution. That means that no solution is acceptable until both people feel they have been part of the decision. When we don't have a win-win, we are left with a win-lose or lose-lose scenario. When emotions kick in, we may leave with one of those outcomes, but no one has really "won". In a win-lose scenario, someone "wins", but there's a price to pay. The person who "lost" is going to carry that, and it often plays out negatively in relationships. It also shows the person who "won" that they can get their way at the expense of their partner. In some situations, this is unavoidable, but it can create a very poor dynamic over time and erode relationships.

Express Appreciation: Regularly express gratitude and appreciation for your partner. Recognize and acknowledge their efforts, both big and small, which can strengthen the emotional bond between you. It's amazing how this simple concept can get lost in relationships. I constantly have patients tell me that they don't feel appreciated by their partner. There are a number of ways this can happen. One is that some people are not good at expressing gratitude. They can improve in this area by being shown appreciation and discussing how important it is for both people to hear.

Another way appreciation gets unfelt is in the form it is expressed. Sadly, we all have some level of expectations of our partners. This means we look for things to be expressed in a certain way. When they aren't, we are disappointed. Our partner may be expressing gratitude in a different way, but it gets missed because it's not in the form we are looking for. This is a responsibility for both people and it happens through communication. To get past this, it's important to discuss what works for each person and try to find a middle ground that works for both.

Set Boundaries: Establish and respect personal boundaries. Clearly communicate your needs and expectations, and encourage your partner to do the same. This helps create a sense of safety and mutual understanding. This concept is getting more difficult with technology playing such a significant role in our lives. How people use cell phones and social media in their relationships has become increasingly problematic. This is another area where communication is key.

Shared Goals and Values: Identify and discuss shared goals and values. Having common aspirations can create a sense of purpose and unity within the relationship. When my wife and I started dating, this was one of the first things we did. We sat down and discussed what our value systems and goals are. Over time, our values have stayed relatively unchanged, but our goals have moved around quite a lot. Our relationship goals have stayed pretty steady, but our individual goals have changed. Recently, we added two more relationship goals–to cook together and to learn to dance together. We've already started on both.

Quality Time: Invest quality time in your relationship. Dedicate time to connect emotionally and engage in activities that both partners enjoy. This helps nurture the bond between you. I often say that we are married and still dating. There's nothing wrong with "Netflix and chill", but there's something to be said about going out and doing different things together. It's important to celebrate important dates, make time to do things together, and engage in activities that you both enjoy. This is more difficult when you have children, but it is doable.

Adaptability: Be adaptable and open to change. Relationships evolve, and being flexible can help both partners grow together rather than apart. This can be difficult, especially if one, or both of you, are stubborn. Change is often scary to many as it threatens our status quo. If we see change as good, we can stay open to each other evolving.

Learn and Grow Together: Embrace opportunities for personal and collective growth. Attend workshops, read books, or seek counseling together to enhance your understanding of each other and improve your relationship. Many people see counseling as a last ditch effort to save something that is, likely, broken. Instead, it can be seen as something to improve each person and the relationship or even prevent it from becoming broken. Christine and I have gone periodically over the years in order to be a better couple. Workshops are a great way to grow in different ways.

Apologize and Forgive: Acknowledge mistakes, apologize when necessary, and forgive each other. Holding on to grudges can erode the trust and connection within a relationship. It seems that saying "I'm sorry" is one of the most difficult things for many people to do. One of the main reasons is that people often lack the emotional maturity to say it. Instead, they make excuses for why the other person may be upset. It took me a long time to be able to say it. Part of the reason was that saying "I'm sorry" meant that I had hurt Christine in some way, and I did not want to admit that, especially because I rarely do anything to knowingly hurt her. It took me a while to learn that apologizing is about the hurt that she experienced, regardless of my intent, and that's worth recognizing.

On the other hand, many people apologize, but don't correct the behavior. I've always said that the best apology is a change in behavior. The sorry doesn't matter, the correction does. Some people will repeatedly apologize and then keep doing the same thing. No thanks! Other people don't have it in them to apologize, but do actually change because of it. That's much better.

Forgiveness, on the other hand, has its own challenges. Many people forgive, but don't forget. While there's value in that, it's also very difficult to move on with that approach. In relationships, anything that isn't a dealbreaker needs to have a level of forgiveness. At the very least, we need to forgive others if we ever want to be forgiven by others. In trauma situations, forgiveness may be more about the ability to move on rather than it being imparted on the person who harmed us.

Positive Mindset: Cultivate a positive mindset. Focus on the strengths of your relationship and appreciate the positive aspects. A positive attitude can contribute to a healthier and more resilient partnership. A positive mindset is critical in maintaining healthy relationships with others and ourselves. As we've discussed with CBT, the way we think is a choice. That concept pertains to positive or negative. When you think about it, what logical reason is there to think negatively? Negative thinking is a literal cancer for our own well-being as well as our relationships. Many people justify negative thinking as realism or some type of defense mechanism, but I have yet to hear a scenario where it works. We'll discuss this at more length in the next chapter.

Remember, the power to improve a relationship is a shared responsibility. Both partners play a role in creating a positive and fulfilling connection. Open communication, mutual respect, and a commitment to growth are foundational elements in building and maintaining a strong relationship. The most important relationship is the one we have with ourself. When we are able be comfortable and happy with who we are, we are no longer threatened by the impact of others. When you are truly okay with who you are and how you feel, no one can make not okay. True power is being who you are, not who you think others want you to be.

Chapter 4

PUTTING EVERYTHING ON THE TABLE

"We cannot change, we cannot move away from what we are, until we thoroughly accept what we are. Then change seems to come about almost unnoticed."
— Carl Rogers

I had a patient who was in and out of jail for many years for various bad crimes. He stopped being compliant with his supervision and missed treatment, which was unusual for him. After being in jail again, he returned to me for sessions. When I asked him why he didn't reach out when he was experiencing a bad turn, he explained it was because he couldn't face me. He said I was the ideal self that he strived to be, and he couldn't sit with me when his real self was so far from that. He was describing Carol Rogers' theory in a very cool way.

The Real Self

Carl Rogers was a prominent American psychologist and one of the founders of humanistic psychology. He introduced the concept of the "ideal self" as part of his theory on personality and self-concept. According to Rogers, individuals have two main components to their self-concept: the "real self" and the "ideal self."

The real self is the actual, current perception that an individual has of themselves. It includes how a person views their personality, abilities, and characteristics. It is based on their real experiences, self-awareness, and self-perception. Rogers introduced the concept of the "real self" as a fundamental aspect of his theory on personality and self-concept within humanistic psychology. The real self represents the actual, current perception that an individual has of themselves. Here are key points related to Rogers' concept of the real self:

Actual Perception: The real self is based on an individual's current, lived experiences and their perception of who they are at a given moment. It includes an awareness of one's thoughts, feelings, behaviors, and personal attributes.

Self-Exploration: Rogers emphasized the importance of self-exploration in developing an accurate understanding of the real self. This involves introspection and an honest examination of one's thoughts, emotions, and behaviors.

Subjective Experience: The real self is subjective and personal. It is the individual's own perception of their identity, influenced by their unique life experiences, relationships, and self-awareness.

Dynamic and Fluid: The real self is not static; it is dynamic and can evolve over time. As individuals experience new things, learn, and grow, their perception of the real self may change.

Congruence with Experience: Rogers believed that psychological health and well-being are associated with congruence between the real self and experience. When there is a match between one's self-perception and actual experiences, it contributes to a sense of authenticity and inner harmony.

Incongruence and Discrepancy: In cases where there is a significant incongruence between the real self and experience, individuals may experience emotional distress, anxiety, or dissatisfaction. Rogers considered this incongruence a central factor in psychological problems.

Role of the Therapist: In the context of person-centered therapy, which Rogers developed, the therapist plays a supportive role in creating an environment conducive to self-exploration. Unconditional positive regard, empathy, and genuine understanding are essential components of the therapeutic relationship.

Development of the Real Self: The development of the real self involves ongoing self-reflection, self-acceptance, and a willingness to engage in personal growth. Rogers believed that individuals have an innate drive towards self-actualization, or becoming the best version of themselves.

In summary, Carl Rogers' concept of the real self underscores the importance of individuals gaining a clear and honest understanding of their current self-perception based on their experiences and self-reflection. The dynamic interaction between the real self and the external world influences psychological well-being and personal growth.

The Ideal Self

The ideal self represents who an individual wishes to become or the qualities, values, and attributes they aspire to possess. It is an idealized version of oneself and is influenced by societal expectations, cultural norms, and personal goals. The ideal self reflects the person someone wants to be in the future.

Carl Rogers introduced the concept of the "ideal self" as part of his humanistic psychology theory on personality and self-concept. The ideal self represents an individual's vision or aspiration of the person they want to become, incorporating their values, goals, and desired qualities. Here are key points related to Rogers' concept of the ideal self:

Future-oriented Vision: The ideal self is a forward-looking concept that represents an individual's vision of their future self. It includes the qualities, characteristics, and achievements that a person aspires to develop or attain.

Aspirations and Goals: Individuals form their ideal self based on personal aspirations, goals, and societal influences. This concept is shaped by cultural norms, societal expectations, and the individual's unique values and desires.

Influence on Motivation: The ideal self serves as a powerful motivator. As individuals strive to align their actual experiences and behaviors with their ideal self, it can drive personal growth, self-improvement, and the pursuit of meaningful goals.

Subjective and Personal: Like the real self, the ideal self is subjective and personal. It reflects an individual's unique perspective on what they consider to be their best or most authentic self.

Alignment with Values: The ideal self is often aligned with an individual's core values and beliefs. Rogers emphasized the importance of authenticity and congruence, encouraging individuals to work towards goals that are consistent with their values.

Continuous Development: The ideal self is not a fixed or static concept. It evolves as individuals grow, learn, and gain new experiences. As goals are achieved or revised, the ideal self adapts accordingly.

Striving for Congruence: Rogers believed that psychological health and well-being are associated with the congruence or alignment between the real self and the ideal self. Striving to close the gap between these two aspects contributes to a sense of self-actualization.

Role in Personal Growth: The ideal self plays a crucial role in personal growth and self-actualization. Rogers viewed the ongoing process of moving towards one's ideal self as essential for psychological well-being.

In summary, Carl Rogers' concept of the ideal self highlights the importance of having a future-oriented vision that guides individuals in their pursuit of personal and psychological growth. The dynamic interaction between the real self and the ideal self contributes to the ongoing development and maturation of an individual's self-concept.

Rogers believed that a healthy and fulfilling life involves a congruence or alignment between the real self and the ideal self. When there is a significant gap between these two aspects of the self, individuals may experience feelings of incongruence, anxiety, and dissatisfaction.

The process of personal growth and self-actualization, according to Rogers, involves moving towards greater congruence between the real self and the ideal self. This occurs through self-exploration, self-acceptance, and working towards personal goals that are in harmony with one's values and aspirations.

Rogers emphasized the importance of unconditional positive regard and empathy in creating a supportive environment for individuals to explore and accept their real selves. He believed that a non-judgmental and accepting atmosphere facilitates personal growth and helps individuals move closer to their ideal self.

Great concept, right? The answer is really simple. Be the person that you want to be. This means, create the vision and then be it. When I discuss this with my kids, I tell them to fake it to make it. This saying is usually associated with being phony and manipulative. Here's a different way to look at it. The ideal self is different from the real self and *we are* our real self. We are looking to be a different person (somewhat) when we strive to become our ideal self. This means we have to behave and think like someone else. The more we "act" like that person, the more we become that person. It's not natural until it is.

Achieving Your Ideal Self

So, how do you get to be your ideal self? Achieving your ideal self involves a process of self-discovery, personal growth, and aligning your actions with your aspirations. Here are some steps to help you work towards your ideal self:

Self-Reflection: Take time for self-reflection to understand your values, goals, and aspirations. Consider what qualities and achievements are important to you in becoming your ideal self. This whole process is very individualistic and involves a lot of looking at yourself. As much as it's important to be aware and considerate of others, we can lose ourselves by thinking too much about what other people think of us. With that said, there is value in focusing on others. Many of my values and goals are based on what I've seen in others.

Years ago, I gave a speech at my children's Cub Scout Blue and Gold Ceremony. In the speech, I explained to the scouts that I have spent much of my life stealing from others. I've stolen mannerisms, ideas, and qualities that spoke to me and which I wanted to emulate. There is a saying that we don't always remember what people say, but we remember how they made us feel. I seek and try to copy the things that people have said and done that made me feel good. Self-reflection is crucial in assessing how we're doing, as well as, what we want to do.

Define Your Values: Clarify your core values. Your ideal self should be aligned with the values that are most important to you. This alignment can provide a strong foundation for your journey toward self-improvement. It's fascinating to me how universal our ideal values are. I speak with patients from all walks of life and ask them what values are important to them, and there is a significant overlap in responses. This becomes more apparent when looking at questions like, "What kind of partner, parent, or friend do you want to be?" It's so important to establish for ourselves what values we think are important and what that looks like in our thoughts and actions.

Set Clear Goals: Define specific and realistic goals that reflect your ideal self. One of my favorite sayings is, "A goal without a plan is just a wish." Any time we want to drive somewhere, we need to know the directions. If we don't have them, it's very unlikely that we will get there. Break down these goals into smaller, manageable steps. Clear goals provide a roadmap for your personal development. I've been "writing" this book for years, but this year is the first time I wrote down the steps, with timeframes, to actually write it.

Create a Vision Board: Consider creating a vision board that visually represents your ideal self. Use images, quotes, and symbols that resonate with your aspirations. Place the vision board in a visible place as a daily reminder. In general, it's really good to surround yourself with visual reminders of what embodies your values and goals. The more concrete you are with yourself, the better. Arnold Schwarzenegger has always been a model for me as he represents commitment to health, goals, and unyielding determination. Naturally, that means that I have a poster of Arnold to keep that visual reminder. My son, Dylan, took my favorite one, so I had to get another one. It's great that he liked the message as much as I did.

Develop Action Plans: Break down your goals into actionable steps. Create detailed action plans that outline the tasks, timelines, and resources needed to move closer to your ideal self. This idea sounds more complicated than it actually is. I have patients who say they want to have their own place by next year. Some have a job and a budget with a set saving plan. Others don't have a job or saving plan. It's pretty easy math to see who has a better chance. For those who are not taking action, we break down the actual process. We start by figuring out how much they will need to move into an apartment and a realistic timeframe to save that amount. For example, if you have 12 months to save $6000, that means saving $500 a month or $125 a week. Once we have the numbers, we discuss how to do realistically save that amount per week.

Embrace Growth Mindset: Adopt a growth mindset that embraces challenges, learning, and resilience. See setbacks as opportunities for growth rather than obstacles. Focus on continuous improvement. Socrates once said, "True knowledge exists in knowing that you know nothing." As dismal as that sounds, accepting it opens us up to learning. Being open to our lack of knowledge is crucial to our growth. This can be difficult when it comes to areas that we know about, but there is always more to know. We never know it all, and those that say they do, don't.

One day, Dylan and I went to a very nerdy collectible store and saw a good friend of mine there. He's a car guy, I never took him for a comic book guy. As it turned out, he's not, but his friend worked there so he was hanging out. He asked me about the different things I was looking at and had follow-up questions with genuine interest. It felt good to talk about something I enjoy to someone who wanted to learn about it.

I learned a very important concept that day. If you want to see the value of anything, learn about it from someone who is passionate about it. You will likely see the beauty and merit of things that we pass by every day. This really opens your brain to learning about everything around you and gaining a fuller appreciation. It's also nice to see people glow when discussing topics that are important and meaningful to them.

Learn and Develop Skills: Identify the skills and knowledge required to embody your ideal self. Invest time in learning and developing these skills through courses, workshops, or mentorship. We often like this concept but never have time. Whenever I hear the time excuse, I always show Arnold's video on YouTube. It's a two-minute clip called "Sleep faster". Watch it now and then come back to the book.

See? Wasn't that worth it? Arnold simplifies and counters the classic excuse of "I have no time." Once you realize that you have sixteen (or eighteen) hours in a day to achieve your goals, then failing to do so is simply poor time choices. If you really want to be honest with yourself, look at your phone and see how much screen time you spend each day. The average amount of screen time is about three and a half hours per day. How much of that time was on purposeful activities? Usually, not that much. Time is like money and calories. By keeping track of your use, you can better control how much you have and how much you use. The results speak for themselves.

Seek Feedback: Request feedback from trusted friends, family, or mentors. They can offer valuable insights into your strengths, areas for improvement, and whether your actions align with your vision of the ideal self. This is something we often avoid, as we may not like what we hear. People may also tell us what they think we want to hear, instead of being honest. Honest feedback is a gift and should be something we seek. As we've discussed before, it's good if it feels bad. Without discomfort, we can't have change or growth. Ironically, we often know the answers to the questions we ask. It's the same process as solving our own problems: if this was someone else's problem, what would your advice be?

In therapy sessions, this is my cheat question. Whenever someone asks me for an answer, I ask what their advice would be in my position. People often answer easily and with insight. This works because we are clouded by emotion when it's our issue. When we look at someone else's issue, we are able to see with logic. If our advice is different from what we are doing, or willing to do, then we are clearly lost in emotion. Making the problem someone else's helps us remove the wall of emotion. This is another simple concept that is difficult for many people to apply.

Cultivate Positive Habits: Develop positive habits that contribute to your personal and professional growth. Whether it's practicing gratitude, maintaining a healthy lifestyle, or enhancing your communication skills, habits play a crucial role in shaping your identity. This is where you fake it to make it. If you are looking to apply behaviors that are not habits yet, you are going to be acting in a way that is not natural or organic, at first. Through repetition, it will become a habit.

I used to brag about things that I did, and it never felt right. It stemmed from wanting to be recognized for doing good things and was based on an insecurity of not feeling seen. This could be due to being the youngest of four and feeling like the forgotten child. Looking for recognition for good deeds partially defeats the positivity of doing something good. When I realized this, I wanted to be more humble. I've seen humility in other people and always respected it. By seeing it in others, I was able to see behaviors that I wanted to copy. In my case, this meant not making a point of telling people when I did something. It's a simple concept, and I'm still working on it. Hopefully, I'm humbler than in the past, but it's still something I'm working on.

Adapt and Revise: Be open to adapting your goals and vision as you grow and evolve. Life circumstances and personal experiences may influence your aspirations, and it's important to revise your vision accordingly.

Celebrate Achievements: Celebrate your achievements, no matter how small. Recognize and appreciate the progress you make toward your ideal self. Positive reinforcement can motivate continued effort.

Practice Self-Compassion: Be kind to yourself during the journey. Acknowledge that growth takes time, and setbacks are a natural part of the process. Practice self-compassion and maintain a positive attitude.

Stay the Course

Remember that the journey toward your ideal self is ongoing and iterative. Embrace the process of self-discovery and growth, and be patient with yourself as you work towards aligning your actions with your vision of the person you aspire to become. As with any destination, it's about the journey. As long as you are on the path, and stay on it, celebrate that you are staying the course. Realistically, we never get to our ideal self, but we should never stop working towards it. It's just like dieting or exercising. We rarely get to where we want, but always feel better when we are doing the work. Sure, we're often hungry when we're dieting, but we have a better chance of getting results than if we stop.

It's important to note that Carl Rogers' ideas have had a significant influence on counseling and psychotherapy. His client-centered therapy, also known as person-centered therapy, is based on the principles of empathy, unconditional positive regard, and congruence in the therapeutic relationship to help individuals explore and reconcile their real and ideal selves. We're going to move away from Carl for several chapters and delve into some of the heavier issues many people face when growing up.

We often need to look back in order to move forward. In the past, I didn't subscribe to this idea. I felt the past is the past, and holding on to negative holds no value. Over time, I learned that it's not realistic to just "let it go". We have to actually do some work in order to get to that outcome. I often say, if we don't deal with our past, it deals with us. The same can be said about feelings or issues. I wanted to start with the Rogers' perspective to keep hope and direction before digging into some of the more negative issues. Don't worry, though, we'll come back to our ideal self after we help our inner child.

Chapter 5

SUBSTANCE USE VERSUS SUBSTANCE ABUSE

"You probably had fantasies about leaving home, about running away, about having it over with, about your alcoholic parent becoming sober and life being fine and beautiful. You began to live in a fairy-tale world, with fantasy and in dreams. You lived a lot on hope, because you didn't want to believe what was happening. You knew that you couldn't talk about it with your friends or adults outside your family. Because you believed you had to keep these feelings to yourself, you learned to keep most of your other feelings to yourself. You couldn't let the rest of the world know what was going on in your home. Who would believe you, anyway?"
– Janet Geringer Woititz

In my career, I've worked with many people who have sold drugs. As can be expected, a lot of them justified their motivation to sell drugs as a financial decision to provide for their families. The more honest answer for most is that they did it because they wanted to. They liked the money, the ease of doing so, the "respect" they got from others, etc. In their justifying, they chose to give in to a common cognitive distortion that they weren't hurting anyone. One person I worked with was confronted with the reality of his choices. For the story, I'll call him Dave.

While Dave was in jail for selling drugs, his daughter refused to call him. When he was released, she contacted him to tell him that he was a grandfather. He found them living in an abandoned building with her drug-addicted mother. He took his daughter and granddaughter to live with him and his wife. He cried for a week straight for them after finally seeing the real consequences of his past lifestyle.

In the past, he chose to ignore the possible impact he was having on people's lives. It's a distortion I've heard from many drug dealers over the years. They justify their actions by saying they didn't make anyone use drugs and that they are going to buy drugs anyway, so what's the difference where they get them from? He now wanted to harm the person who was selling his daughter's mother drugs. As you can imagine, part of that anger was towards himself as he was the person who sold drugs to someone else's mother, daughter, son, etc.

There are many layers to a story like this. We have Dave's history that led to him being a drug dealer. He didn't have a significant history of drug use, but grew up "in the streets" and was drawn to the wrong influences. He saw every stage of drug use and abuse while engaged in that lifestyle. He chose partners who were aware of his criminal behavior and, for their own reasons, chose to be with him. His daughters grew up with their father being in and out of jail and not being present. These factors have a number of possible effects on development. Dave's first daughter's mother had her own addiction issues, which led to her daughter trying to take care of her mother and her young child.

It's easy to look at Dave and his story and wonder why would anyone live like this. This question is asked a lot when looking at families with extreme conditions. The answer usually lies in understanding the frog in the pot. Let me explain. I had a colleague who gave a really good analogy. If you put a frog in a pot of water, the frog will likely swim in the water and enjoy the experience. If you put the frog in a pot of boiling water, it will likely jump out of the water to avoid dying. However, if the frog starts in the regular water and the water is gradually heated, the frog will keep adjusting to the heat until the water boils and the frog dies. The point is, when you look at someone's crisis, including our own, it's important to realize that it probably didn't start that way. It should teach us to be aware of change and respond lest the change lead to worse outcomes. This leads us into understanding when "use" becomes "abuse".

Over the years, society has used the terms "alcoholic" and "addict". These terms help us try to understand a problem by naming it, but there is a subjectivity to these words. It may be more helpful to try to figure out when something is a problem. A problem may be defined by determining if something is more important to you than what's supposed to be important. I often use the example of peanut butter. Peanut butter is not a drug and it is not illegal. If you like peanut butter so much that you miss work because you have to stay home and eat it, then it's a problem. If eating peanut butter is creating issues in your relationships, then it's a problem. If your doctor tells you that you're having health issues from eating too much peanut butter, then it's a problem. I'm sure you can see where this is headed. Anything can be considered "abuse" when it's a problem.

This is an easier discussion when looking at alcohol, since it isn't illegal and is considered socially acceptable. In many states, marijuana now fits in the same category. Illegal drugs could, and many would argue should, fit easily into this concept. Anything that could result in being arrested would certainly get in the way of most other things that are important to us. People have argued that "lightly" using illegal drugs is recreational and not problematic. That's just an excuse to do something that is knowingly wrong. In psychology, we call it rationalization.

Research can often present differing takes on various topics. The following part is more indicative of some of the more recent take on illegal drugs. Some of it differs from the more concrete idea of legal versus illegal. The terms "substance use" and "substance abuse" refer to different patterns of behavior related to the consumption of psychoactive substances. These terms are often used in the context of understanding the impact of substance use on an individual's health, well-being, and overall functioning. Below is a brief distinction between the two.

Substance Use

Definition: Substance use refers to the act of consuming psychoactive substances, including alcohol and drugs, for various purposes, such as relaxation, recreation, socialization, or medicinal reasons.

Behavioral Context: Not all substance use is problematic or indicative of a substance use disorder. Many people use substances in a controlled and responsible manner without experiencing negative consequences.

Substance Abuse

Definition: Substance abuse is a more specific and clinical term that is used when an individual's substance use becomes harmful, hazardous, or leads to negative consequences in their life. It implies a pattern of use that is detrimental to the person's physical health, mental well-being, relationships, work, or other areas of functioning.

Diagnostic Criteria: Substance abuse is often diagnosed as a substance use disorder, which is classified in the Diagnostic and Statistical Manual of Mental Disorders (DSM-5). To be diagnosed with a substance use disorder, an individual must meet specific criteria related to the severity of their substance-related problems.

Basically, "substance use" is a broad term encompassing any use of psychoactive substances, while "substance abuse" specifically refers to a problematic pattern of use associated with negative consequences. The severity and impact of substance use are key factors in determining whether it falls into the category of substance abuse or a diagnosed substance use disorder. It's important to note that not everyone who uses substances engages in substance abuse, and identifying problematic patterns early on allows for preventive measures and appropriate interventions.

Substance abuse, also referred to as substance use disorder, is a condition characterized by the harmful or hazardous use of psychoactive substances, including alcohol and illicit drugs. It involves the inability to control or stop the use of these substances despite negative consequences on one's health, relationships, work, or other aspects of life. Substance abuse can have serious physical, psychological, and social implications.

Key aspects of substance abuse

Types of Substances: Substance abuse can involve various types of substances, including alcohol, prescription medications, illegal drugs (such as cocaine, heroin, and methamphetamine), and other substances that have the potential for misuse.

Alcohol

Alcohol use and abuse represent two different patterns of behavior related to the consumption of alcohol. It's important to differentiate between moderate, responsible alcohol use, and problematic alcohol abuse, which may lead to serious health, social, and psychological consequences.

Alcohol Use Definition: Alcohol use refers to the consumption of alcoholic beverages in a controlled and responsible manner. It encompasses social drinking, moderate consumption, and occasional use.

Behavioral Context: Many individuals use alcohol without experiencing negative consequences. Moderate alcohol consumption is generally considered safe for most adults and may even have some potential health benefits, particularly with certain types of alcohol like red wine.

Alcohol Abuse Definition: Alcohol abuse, also known as alcohol misuse, refers to a pattern of drinking that leads to negative consequences. It involves behaviors such as binge-drinking, heavy drinking, or drinking in situations where it poses a risk to health and safety.

Diagnostic Criteria: Alcohol abuse is often diagnosed as part of an alcohol use disorder (AUD), a clinical term used in the Diagnostic and Statistical Manual of Mental Disorders (DSM-5). To receive a diagnosis of an AUD, an individual must meet specific criteria related to the severity of their alcohol-related problems.

Key Differences

Control and Consequences: Alcohol use is characterized by controlled and responsible drinking without significant negative consequences. In contrast, alcohol abuse involves drinking patterns that result in adverse effects on health, relationships, work, or other areas of life.

Frequency and Intensity: Alcohol use may involve moderate and occasional consumption. Alcohol abuse typically includes patterns of excessive, frequent, or dangerous drinking that may lead to physical or psychological harm.

Awareness and Adaptability: Individuals engaging in alcohol use are generally aware of their limits and can adapt their drinking behavior to different social contexts. In alcohol abuse, there may be a lack of awareness, control, or adaptability, leading to continued problematic behavior.

It's important to note that the transition from alcohol use to alcohol abuse can be gradual, and early intervention is crucial to prevent the development of more severe problems. If someone is concerned about their alcohol consumption or that of a loved one, seeking professional help from healthcare providers, counselors, or support groups can provide assistance and guidance in addressing alcohol-related issues.

Marijuana

Marijuana use and abuse refer to different patterns of behavior related to the consumption of marijuana, a psychoactive substance derived from the cannabis plant. While marijuana is used for various purposes, including medicinal and recreational, its misuse or abuse can lead to health and social consequences. Here's a distinction between marijuana use and abuse:

Marijuana Use Definition: Marijuana use involves the responsible and controlled consumption of marijuana for various purposes, such as medicinal, recreational, or religious reasons.

Behavioral Context: Individuals who use marijuana responsibly adhere to local laws, regulations, and cultural norms related to its use. Medicinal use is often prescribed by healthcare professionals to manage certain medical conditions, such as chronic pain or nausea.

Marijuana Abuse Definition: Marijuana abuse, also known as cannabis use disorder, occurs when individuals engage in problematic patterns of marijuana consumption that lead to negative consequences in various aspects of their lives.

Behavioral Context: Marijuana abuse can involve using larger amounts than intended, unsuccessful attempts to cut down or control use, spending a significant amount of time obtaining or using marijuana, neglecting responsibilities due to marijuana use, and continued use despite knowledge of adverse effects.

Key Differences

Purpose of Use: Marijuana use can be for various purposes, including relaxation, recreation, creativity, pain management, and medicinal purposes. Abuse often involves using marijuana for nonmedical and recreational purposes in a way that leads to negative consequences.

Control and Consequences: Marijuana use is characterized by controlled and responsible consumption without significant negative consequences. Marijuana abuse involves patterns of use that result in adverse effects on health, relationships, work, or other areas of life.

Frequency and Intensity: Marijuana use may involve moderate and occasional consumption, depending on the purpose. Marijuana abuse typically includes patterns of excessive, frequent, or compulsive use that may lead to physical or psychological harm.

Legal and Cultural Context: Marijuana use may occur within legal and cultural frameworks, such as areas where it is legalized for recreational or medicinal use. Marijuana abuse may involve behaviors that violate legal regulations or cultural norms surrounding its use.

It's important to note that attitudes toward marijuana use vary globally, and legalization status varies across different jurisdictions. While some individuals use marijuana responsibly for medicinal or recreational purposes, others may develop problematic patterns of use that warrant attention and intervention. If individuals are concerned about their marijuana use or that of someone they know, seeking guidance from healthcare professionals or addiction specialists is recommended.

Prescription Medication

Prescription medication use and abuse refer to different patterns of behavior related to the consumption of medications prescribed by a healthcare professional. While prescription medications can provide therapeutic benefits when used as directed, their misuse or abuse can lead to serious health consequences. Here's a distinction between prescription medication use and abuse:

Prescription Medication Use Definition: Prescription medication use involves taking medications as prescribed by a licensed healthcare professional to address specific health conditions. This includes following the recommended dosage, frequency, and duration outlined by the healthcare provider.

Behavioral Context: When individuals use prescription medications as directed by their healthcare provider to manage medical conditions, it is considered appropriate use. This can include medications for pain management, mental health, chronic conditions, and other health issues.

Prescription Medication Abuse Definition: Prescription medication abuse, also known as nonmedical use, occurs when individuals use prescription medications in ways other than prescribed by a healthcare professional. This includes taking higher doses, using medications without a prescription, or using them for recreational purposes.

Behavioral Context: Prescription medication abuse can involve taking medications to achieve a desired effect, such as euphoria, sedation, or altered perception. This behavior can lead to serious health risks, dependence, and addiction.

Key Differences

Medical Necessity: Prescription medication use is driven by medical necessity, where individuals take medications to address specific health conditions under the guidance of a healthcare professional. In contrast, prescription medication abuse involves using medications for nonmedical or recreational purposes.

Dosage and Frequency: Prescription medication use involves adhering to the prescribed dosage, frequency, and duration recommended by a healthcare provider. In prescription medication abuse, individuals may exceed recommended doses, take medications more frequently than prescribed, or use them in ways not intended by the healthcare provider.

Health Consequences: Proper prescription medication use is intended to improve or manage health conditions, leading to positive health outcomes. Prescription medication abuse can result in adverse effects, increased risk of overdose, physical and psychological dependence, and other health complications.

Legality and Safety: Prescription medication use is legal when done under the supervision of a licensed healthcare professional. Prescription medication abuse often involves the illegal acquisition or use of medications without a prescription, which poses safety risks.

It's crucial for individuals to use prescription medications responsibly, following the guidance of healthcare providers. If there are concerns about the use of prescription medications, communication with healthcare professionals is essential. Seeking help from healthcare providers, pharmacists, and mental health professionals is important for addressing potential issues related to prescription medication use and abuse.

Illegal Drugs

The terms "illegal drug use" and "drug abuse" refer to different patterns of behavior related to the consumption of drugs, specifically those substances that are prohibited by law. Understanding the distinctions between these terms is important for discussions about public health, substance use disorders, and law enforcement efforts. It should be clear from the themes of this book that any illegal behavior is ill-advised and usually indicates problems in one or more areas. For literary and clinical purposes, here's a breakdown of the concepts:

Illegal Drug Use Definition: Illegal drug use refers to the consumption of substances that are prohibited by law. It includes any use of illicit drugs, such as cocaine, heroin, methamphetamine, ecstasy, LSD, and others, in violation of legal regulations.

Behavioral Context: Individuals engaging in illegal drug use may do so for various reasons, including recreation, experimentation, self-medication, or peer influence. It's important to note that not all drug users develop substance use disorders, and some may use drugs infrequently without experiencing significant negative consequences.

Drug Abuse Definition: Drug abuse involves a problematic pattern of drug use that leads to negative consequences on an individual's health, relationships, work, or other areas of life. It can be associated with the misuse of legal drugs (such as prescription medications) or the use of illegal drugs.

Diagnostic Criteria: Drug abuse is often diagnosed as part of a substance use disorder (SUD) using criteria outlined in the Diagnostic and Statistical Manual of Mental Disorders (DSM-5). To receive a diagnosis of a substance use disorder, an individual must meet specific criteria related to the severity of their drug-related problems.

Key Differences

Legality: Illegal drug use involves the consumption of substances that are prohibited by law. Drug abuse can involve the misuse of legal drugs (e.g., prescription medications) or the use of illicit drugs.

Control and Consequences: Illegal drug use may or may not lead to negative consequences, depending on the individual and the circumstances. Drug abuse involves problematic patterns of use that result in adverse effects on health, relationships, work, or other areas of life.

Diagnostic Criteria: While illegal drug use is a legal term, drug abuse is a clinical concept often diagnosed as part of a substance use disorder. The diagnosis considers the severity of drug-related problems and their impact on an individual's life.

Intent and Frequency: Illegal drug use encompasses any use of prohibited substances, regardless of intent or frequency. Drug abuse often implies a more chronic and problematic pattern of use that may be associated with dependence, addiction, or harmful consequences.

Addressing issues related to illegal drug use and drug abuse involves a comprehensive approach that includes prevention, education, healthcare interventions, and law enforcement efforts. Individuals struggling with drug-related issues are encouraged to seek help from healthcare professionals, addiction specialists, or support groups.

Signs and Symptoms: Signs of substance abuse can vary depending on the substance but may include changes in behavior, neglect of responsibilities, physical health issues, legal problems, social withdrawal, and an increasing tolerance to the substance, leading to higher consumption.

Risk Factors: Certain factors can contribute to the development of substance abuse, including genetic predisposition, family history of substance use disorders, environmental factors, mental health conditions, trauma, and societal influences.

Physical and Mental Health Impact: Substance abuse can lead to a range of physical health issues, including cardiovascular problems, liver damage, respiratory issues, and an increased risk of infectious diseases. It is also associated with mental health disorders such as anxiety, depression, and substance-induced psychosis.

Tolerance and Dependence: Regular substance abuse often leads to tolerance, where individuals require larger amounts of the substance to achieve the desired effect. Dependence can develop, leading to withdrawal symptoms when substance use is reduced or stopped.

Impact on Relationships: Substance abuse can strain relationships with family, friends, and colleagues. It may lead to conflicts, breakdowns in communication, and isolation as individuals prioritize substance use over their interpersonal connections.

Legal Consequences: Substance abuse can result in legal consequences, including arrests and convictions related to possession, distribution, or impaired driving under the influence of substances.

Treatment Options: Treatment for substance abuse typically involves a combination of behavioral therapy, counseling, and, in some cases, medication. Detoxification may be necessary for certain substances with withdrawal symptoms.

Recovery and Relapse: Recovery from substance abuse is a complex process that requires ongoing commitment and support. Relapse, or a return to substance use after a period of abstinence, is a common challenge, but it does not signify failure. It often indicates the need for adjustments to the treatment plan.

Prevention: Prevention efforts focus on education, raising awareness, and addressing risk factors. Early intervention and education about the consequences of substance abuse can help prevent its onset.

It's important for individuals struggling with substance abuse to seek professional help. Substance use disorders are treatable, and recovery is possible with the right support and interventions. If you or someone you know is facing substance abuse issues, consider reaching out to healthcare professionals, counselors, or addiction specialists for assistance.

Effects of Substance Abuse

Substance abuse can have profound and far-reaching impacts on families, affecting the emotional, psychological, social, and economic well-being of all family members. The consequences can vary depending on the severity and duration of the substance abuse, but common effects include:

Breakdown of Communication: Substance abuse often leads to a breakdown in communication within the family. Trust may be eroded, and open, honest communication becomes challenging. Family members may avoid discussing the issue, contributing to a sense of isolation and frustration.

Emotional Distress: Family members may experience a range of emotions, including anxiety, fear, anger, guilt, and sadness. Witnessing a loved one's struggle with substance abuse can be emotionally distressing, leading to mental health challenges for all family members.

Codependency: Codependency may develop, where family members unintentionally enable the substance abuser's behavior by making excuses, covering up for them, or minimizing the impact of their actions. This dynamic can perpetuate the cycle of substance abuse.

Financial Strain: Substance abuse can lead to financial difficulties due to increased spending on substances, legal issues, and potential job loss. The financial strain can affect the entire family, impacting housing, education, and basic needs.

Role Reversal: The roles within the family may become disrupted as family members take on new responsibilities to compensate for the substance abuser's inability to fulfill their roles. Children, in particular, may take on caregiving roles beyond their years.

Family Conflict: Substance abuse can contribute to heightened levels of conflict within the family. Arguments may arise over the substance abuser's behavior, responsibilities, and the impact on family life. Conflict can lead to a hostile and tense family environment.

Childhood Trauma: Children in families affected by substance abuse may experience childhood trauma, witnessing unpredictable and chaotic behavior. This can have long-term effects on their emotional and psychological well-being, potentially leading to a cycle of substance abuse in the next generation.

Social Isolation: Families dealing with substance abuse may experience social isolation as they may withdraw from social activities to avoid judgment or stigmatization. This isolation can further exacerbate feelings of shame and contribute to a lack of support.

Legal Issues: Substance abuse can lead to legal problems, such as arrests for possession or driving under the influence. Legal issues can compound the stress on the family and have long-term consequences for the substance abuser and their loved ones.

Health Consequences: The substance abuser's health may deteriorate, leading to additional stress and concerns for the family. Health problems may require increased caregiving and medical expenses.

Addressing the impact of substance abuse on families often requires a multifaceted approach, including counseling, support groups, and rehabilitation programs. Seeking professional help for both the substance abuser and affected family members is essential to breaking the cycle of substance abuse and fostering healing within the family unit.

Growing Up With Substance Abuse

If you grew up experiencing substance abuse, it's important to learn and heal from it. After all, that's the point of this book. Growing up in an environment with substance abuse can have a profound impact on an individual's well-being. This is one of the most important sections of this chapter, so please consider each point if this applies to you. If you experienced such an upbringing, here are some steps you can consider to address the effects and work towards a healthier life:

Acknowledge and Understand the Impact: Recognize and understand the impact that growing up with substance abuse may have had on your life. This acknowledgment is an essential first step in the process of healing and self-awareness.

Seek Professional Help: Consider seeking support from mental health professionals, counselors, or therapists. They can help you navigate the emotional and psychological challenges associated with growing up in a substance-abusing environment.

Join Support Groups: Connect with support groups or organizations that focus on individuals who have experienced similar challenges. Sharing your experiences and hearing from others can provide a sense of community, understanding, and validation.

Establish Healthy Boundaries: Learn to establish and maintain healthy boundaries in your relationships. Understand the importance of setting limits to protect your well-being and avoid enabling harmful behavior.

Educate Yourself: Educate yourself about the effects of substance abuse and addiction. Understanding the nature of the problem can help you make informed decisions and overcome any misconceptions or stigmas associated with it.

Develop Coping Strategies: Work on developing healthy coping strategies to deal with stress, anxiety, and other challenges. This may involve mindfulness, meditation, exercise, or engaging in activities that bring you joy and relaxation.

Build a Support Network: Surround yourself with a supportive network of friends, family, or mentors who understand your experiences and are committed to your well-being. These individuals can offer encouragement, guidance, and emotional support.

Consider Therapy or Counseling: Participate in individual or group therapy to explore and address the emotional impact of growing up in a substance-abusing environment. Therapists can help you develop coping mechanisms and strategies for personal growth.

Break the Cycle: Be intentional about breaking any negative cycles or patterns that may have been perpetuated by the substance abuse in your upbringing. This may involve making conscious choices to create a different, healthier lifestyle.

Focus on Personal Growth: Invest time and effort in personal growth. Set goals, pursue education or career opportunities, and engage in activities that contribute to your overall well-being and fulfillment.

Practice Self-Care: Prioritize self-care by taking care of your physical, emotional, and mental health. This includes getting adequate sleep, maintaining a balanced diet, and engaging in activities that bring you joy and relaxation.

Forgive and Heal: Consider forgiveness as part of your healing process. Forgiving doesn't necessarily mean condoning past actions, but it can free you from the burden of resentment and contribute to your own emotional well-being.

Remember, healing is a gradual process, and seeking professional support is a sign of strength. Each person's journey is unique, so finding strategies and resources that work for you is important in building a healthier and more fulfilling life.

Recognizing a Substance Abuse Problem

Sadly, substance abuse can be part of generational cycles. I was so worried about this possibility, that I didn't drink for most of my twenties. If you've experienced substance abuse, it's important to learn from it so you don't repeat cycles, but also heal from it since the impact can be far-reaching. Experiencing drug or alcohol abuse can be challenging, but there are steps you can take to address the issue and seek help. Here are some suggestions:

Acknowledge the Problem: Recognize and acknowledge that there is a problem with drug or alcohol abuse. Denial can be a significant barrier to seeking help, so being honest with yourself is a crucial first step.

Reach Out for Support: Share your concerns with trusted friends, family members, or colleagues. Seeking emotional support from those close to you can provide a foundation for addressing the issue and making positive changes.

Consult a Healthcare Professional: Schedule an appointment with a healthcare professional, such as a doctor or therapist, to discuss your substance use. They can provide a professional assessment, offer guidance, and recommend appropriate treatment options.

Explore Treatment Options: Investigate different treatment options, including outpatient counseling, inpatient rehabilitation, support groups, and medication-assisted treatment. The appropriate treatment will depend on the severity of the substance use and individual circumstances.

Join Support Groups: Consider joining support groups such as Alcoholics Anonymous (AA) or Narcotics Anonymous (NA). Connecting with others who have faced similar challenges can provide valuable insights, encouragement, and a sense of community.

Engage in Counseling or Therapy: Individual or group counseling can be beneficial in addressing the underlying issues contributing to substance abuse. Therapists can help you develop coping strategies, set goals, and work through emotional challenges.

Create a Supportive Environment: Surround yourself with a supportive environment that encourages positive change. This may involve distancing yourself from negative influences or situations that contribute to substance abuse.

Develop Coping Strategies: Learn and practice healthy coping strategies to manage stress, emotions, and triggers that may contribute to substance abuse. This might include mindfulness, exercise, hobbies, or other constructive activities.

Consider Medication-Assisted Treatment (MAT): For certain substances, medication-assisted treatment may be an appropriate option. This involves the use of medications, under medical supervision, to assist with the recovery process.

Establish a Relapse Prevention Plan: Work with your healthcare professional or therapist to develop a relapse prevention plan. This plan may include identifying triggers, developing coping strategies, and creating a support network to prevent relapse.

Take Steps Toward Lifestyle Changes: Adopt a healthy lifestyle by focusing on proper nutrition, regular exercise, and sufficient sleep. These lifestyle changes can contribute to overall well-being and support recovery.

Celebrate Progress: Celebrate small victories and progress along the way. Recovery is a journey, and acknowledging positive changes can boost motivation and self-esteem.

Remember, seeking help is a sign of strength, and recovery is possible with the right support and resources. If you or someone you know is struggling with drug or alcohol abuse, consider reaching out to healthcare professionals, addiction specialists, or local support organizations to get the assistance needed for a healthier and more fulfilling life.

Chapter 6

UNDERSTANDING ABUSE

"As traumatized children, we always dreamed that
someone would come and save us. We never dreamed
that it would, in fact, be ourselves as adults."
– Alice Little

I had a session with an individual who trafficked females. He was
credibly on a path of reflection and redemption, knowing he can't undo
the hurt he's caused. He described the females he trafficked as "broken".
He believed that for him to be around and attract people who were
broken, he must have been broken too. It's a pretty simple concept–we
attract what we put out. The people around us are reflections of us, so
it's not as simple as changing your company, you have to change yourself
first.

The word "broken" really resonated with me, though. What makes
someone broken? How does one know if they are broken. How does
one become unbroken? To answer the first question, we have to ask if
they were always broken. If yes, then how come? If no, then when did it
happen? Not everyone's problems started with childhood, but the book
does focus on the past, so we'll start there. Even if problems started in
adulthood, a lot of the solutions will be the same since they are present
and future based.

For many years, I had the privilege of teaching child protective
investigations. As unpleasant as the subject is, I felt that by teaching

proper investigations, I was helping children and families in some small way. I also worked with many great people over the years who shared the same goal of protecting children. Since teaching is a form of learning, I was constantly being educated. One important distinction is the difference between abuse and neglect. This chapter will explain the various aspects of both. For the purpose of this book, the language will be less important than understanding what it all means and the various effects that people may experience.

Child Abuse

Child abuse is a tragic and complex issue that involves harming a child physically, emotionally, sexually, or through neglect. It can occur within families, communities, institutions, or even online. Here are some key aspects to understand about child abuse:

Physical Abuse

Physical abuse involves intentionally causing physical harm or injury to a child. This can include hitting, punching, kicking, burning, or any other form of physical violence. In New York, the criterium is that the parent or caretaker caused protracted disfigurement or that their action would have. In other words, they caused permanent damage like scars or breaks.

Forms of Physical Abuse
Hitting and Beating: This involves striking a child with hands or objects such as belts, sticks, or cords, resulting in bruises, cuts, or other injuries.

Shaking: Shaking a child violently can cause severe head injuries, brain damage, or even death, particularly in infants.

Burning: Burning a child with hot objects, liquids, or cigarettes causes physical injuries and leaves scars.

Force-Feeding or Withholding Food: Forcing a child to eat or withholding food as a form of punishment can lead to physical harm and malnutrition.

Any other Form of Physical Violence: This includes any action that causes physical pain or harm to a child, whether through direct physical contact or through other means.

Signs and Symptoms
Physical signs such as bruises, welts, burns, broken bones, or other unexplained injuries.

Changes in behavior such as withdrawal, aggression, fearfulness, or a sudden reluctance to go home or be around certain individuals.

A child may exhibit signs of anxiety, depression, or post-traumatic stress disorder (PTSD).

Poor school performance, frequent absences, or difficulty concentrating may also indicate abuse.

Emotional Abuse

This form of abuse involves behaviors that harm a child's self-esteem, emotional well-being, or social development. It can include verbal abuse, threats, intimidation, rejection, or constant criticism.

Forms of Emotional Abuse
Verbal Abuse: This includes yelling, shouting, name-calling, belittling, or using derogatory language towards a child.

Threats and Intimidation: Making threats of harm, abandonment, or other forms of punishment to control the child's behavior.

Rejection and Neglect: Withholding affection, attention, or emotional support from the child, or treating them with indifference.

Constant Criticism and Humiliation: Continuously criticizing or ridiculing the child, undermining their self-worth and confidence.

Isolation: Preventing the child from socializing with others, controlling their interactions, or keeping them isolated from supportive relationships.

Exploitation and Manipulation: Using the child for personal gain, manipulating their emotions or beliefs, or exploiting their vulnerabilities for the abuser's benefit.

Signs and Symptoms

Emotional abuse can be more difficult to detect than physical abuse, as it leaves no visible scars. However, there are some signs and symptoms that may indicate emotional abuse:

- Behavioral changes such as withdrawal, aggression, or clinginess.
- Low self-esteem, self-blame, or feelings of worthlessness.
- Anxiety, depression, or other mental health issues.
- Difficulty forming relationships or trusting others.
- Regression in developmental milestones or academic performance.
- Self-harming behaviors or suicidal ideation.

Long-Term Consequences: Emotional abuse can have profound and lasting effects on a child's emotional and psychological well-being. Children who experience emotional abuse are at higher risk of developing mental health issues such as depression, anxiety disorders, PTSD, and problems with emotional regulation. Long-term consequences may include difficulties forming healthy relationships, low self-esteem, self-destructive behaviors, and challenges in academic and social settings.

Sexual Abuse

Sexual abuse involves any form of sexual activity with a child, including molestation, rape, incest, or exploitation. It can also involve exposing a child to sexual content or forcing them to participate in pornography. We'll discuss this at length in later chapters.

Neglect

Neglect occurs when a caregiver fails to provide for a child's basic needs, such as food, shelter, clothing, medical care, education, or emotional support. Neglect accounts for approximately 85%–90% of child protective cases. It can take various forms and can have serious and long-lasting consequences for a child's health and well-being. Here are key points to understand about child neglect:

Forms of Neglect
Physical Neglect: This involves failing to provide for a child's basic physical needs, such as adequate food, clothing, shelter, and supervision. It may also include failing to provide appropriate medical care or treatment for illnesses or injuries.

Educational Neglect: Neglecting a child's educational needs, such as failing to enroll them in school, ensuring regular attendance, or providing necessary support and resources for learning.

Emotional Neglect: This form of neglect occurs when a caregiver fails to provide the emotional support, affection, and nurturing that a child needs for healthy development. It may involve ignoring the child's emotional needs, dismissing their feelings, or subjecting them to emotional abuse.

Medical Neglect: Refusing or delaying necessary medical care for a child's physical or mental health needs, which can result in serious harm or even death.

Signs and Symptoms
Signs of neglect may vary depending on the specific type of neglect, but common indicators include:

- Poor hygiene, unkempt appearance, or inadequate clothing.
- Malnutrition or signs of hunger, such as frequent begging for food or stealing food.
- Lack of appropriate medical care, untreated illnesses or injuries, or frequent absences from school due to health-related issues.

- Developmental delays or academic difficulties due to lack of educational support or stimulation.
- Emotional issues such as low self-esteem, social withdrawal, or difficulty forming relationships.
- In extreme cases, neglect may result in serious health problems, injuries, or fatalities.

Long-Term Consequences: Child neglect can have significant and lasting effects on a child's physical health, emotional well-being, cognitive development, and social functioning. Long-term consequences may include chronic health problems, developmental delays, academic difficulties, behavioral problems, mental health issues, and difficulties forming healthy relationships. Neglected children may also be at increased risk of experiencing further abuse or victimization.

Risk Factors: Certain factors increase the risk of child abuse, including substance abuse, mental illness, poverty, domestic violence, lack of parenting skills, and a history of being abused as a child. Stressful life events such as divorce, unemployment, or housing instability can also contribute to an increased risk of child abuse.

Effects: Child abuse can have profound and long-lasting effects on a child's physical health, emotional well-being, and social development.

Victims of abuse may experience a range of emotional and psychological issues such as depression, anxiety, post-traumatic stress disorder (PTSD), low self-esteem, and difficulty forming healthy relationships. Physical consequences of abuse can include injuries, chronic health problems, and developmental delays. Children who experience abuse may also be at higher risk of engaging in risky behaviors, substance abuse, and juvenile delinquency.

Prevention and Intervention: Preventing child abuse requires a multi-faceted approach that involves education, support services for families, community involvement, and effective policies and legislation. Early intervention is crucial in identifying and addressing instances of abuse. Teachers, healthcare professionals, social workers, and other individuals who work with children play a vital role in recognizing signs of abuse and providing support to victims.

Reporting suspicions of child abuse to the appropriate authorities, such as child protective services or law enforcement, is essential for ensuring the safety and well-being of the child.

Legal and Ethical Considerations: Child abuse is illegal in most jurisdictions, and perpetrators can face criminal charges and imprisonment. There are also ethical considerations surrounding reporting suspected cases of child abuse, as professionals are mandated reporters in many places, meaning they are legally obligated to report suspected abuse or neglect.

It's important for society as a whole to prioritize the protection of children and work together to prevent and address instances of child abuse. Providing support to victims and their families, promoting awareness, and advocating for policies that prioritize child welfare are all critical steps in addressing this issue.

Past Abuse in Adulthood

If I've been abused, how would I know if it's still affecting me? Childhood abuse can have profound and lasting effects on individuals as they transition into adulthood. These effects can be psychological, physical, social, and emotional, impacting almost every aspect of a person's life. Below is an overview of some of the most significant effects.

Psychological Effects

Mental Health Disorders: Adults who experienced childhood abuse are at a higher risk of developing mental health disorders such as depression, anxiety, post-traumatic stress disorder (PTSD), and personality disorders. Some of these disorders can develop for a number of reasons, but if you've experienced abuse, it's a good place to start. As helpful as this book is, don't use it to self-diagnose. It will just help point you in the right direction.

Self-esteem and Self-image Issues: Experiences of abuse can lead to chronic low self-esteem and negative self-image, affecting one's sense of self-worth and confidence. Naturally, good self-esteem is an ongoing challenge for most. If you replay tapes in your head from early experiences and they cause you to question your self-worth, the next chapter will help you start to leave the negative ones behind.

Attachment and Trust Issues: Early abuse can disrupt the normal development of attachment, leading to difficulties in forming healthy relationships and trust issues. It's natural to feel insecure in relationships, and this can result in becoming dependent or jealous. This theme will come up throughout the book. As you work on loving yourself, worrying about what someone else is doing will be less of a threat

Physical Effects

Chronic Health Conditions: There's a correlation between childhood abuse and the development of chronic health conditions in adulthood, such as heart disease, diabetes, and obesity. There's a strong connection between the body and the mind. It's difficult to be physically healthy if we aren't emotionally healthy. Years of poor health habits that were developed as a way of coping or surviving abuse can create long-term health problems.

Neurological Impact: The neurological impact of abuse, particularly during the developmental stages of childhood, can be profound and long-lasting. The brain's structure and function are highly susceptible to environmental influences during its developmental years, making childhood trauma, including abuse, a significant factor in altering brain development. Here's how abuse can affect the neurological development and functioning:

Altered Brain Development
Structural Changes: Research has shown that exposure to abuse can lead to changes in the physical structure of the brain. For instance, the hippocampus, which is involved in memory and emotional regulation, may be smaller in individuals who have experienced severe stress or trauma. Similarly, the prefrontal cortex, which is responsible for decision-making, impulse control, and self-regulation, can also be affected.

Amygdala Reactivity: The amygdala, the part of the brain involved in fear and emotional responses, may become hyperreactive in individuals who have experienced abuse. This can lead to heightened stress responses and difficulty regulating emotions.

Impaired Neurological Functioning

Stress Regulation: Childhood abuse can disrupt the body's stress management systems, including the hypothalamic-pituitary-adrenal (HPA) axis, leading to an overactive or dysregulated stress response. This can manifest as anxiety, depression, and difficulties in managing stress.

Cognitive Impacts: Exposure to early trauma can impair cognitive functions, including attention, memory, and executive functioning. This can affect academic performance, occupational success, and daily decision-making.

Emotional Regulation: Individuals who have experienced childhood abuse may have trouble regulating emotions, leading to increased vulnerability to mood disorders, such as depression and anxiety, and difficulties in forming healthy emotional attachments.

Potential for Recovery

Neuroplasticity: The brain's ability to form new neural connections, known as neuroplasticity, offers a potential pathway for recovery. Therapeutic interventions, such as cognitive behavioral therapy (CBT) and trauma-informed therapies, can help mitigate some of the neurological impacts of abuse.

Supportive Environments: Creating supportive, nurturing environments for survivors of childhood abuse can also play a crucial role in healing. Positive relationships and experiences can foster resilience and aid in the recovery of neurological functions affected by trauma.

Understanding the neurological impact of childhood abuse underscores the importance of early intervention and support for individuals who have experienced trauma. With appropriate care, there is potential for significant recovery and improvement in neurological functioning, highlighting the brain's remarkable capacity for resilience and healing.

Behavioral and Social Effects

Relationship Problems: Adults who were abused as children may struggle with forming or maintaining relationships due to trust issues, fear of intimacy, or misunderstanding of healthy boundaries.

Substance Abuse: Some turn to drugs or alcohol as a coping mechanism, leading to substance abuse disorders.

Academic and Occupational Challenges: The impact on cognitive and emotional regulation can affect educational attainment and occupational success.

Emotional Effects

Difficulty Regulating Emotions: Individuals may have heightened responses to stress or difficulty managing emotions due to the lasting impact of abuse.

Fear and Anxiety: Persistent fear, anxiety, and hypervigilance can be common, especially if the abuse was unpredictable or from a caregiver.

Feelings of Worthlessness: Deep-seated feelings of guilt, shame, and worthlessness are prevalent among those who experienced childhood abuse.

It's important to note that these effects can vary significantly from person to person, depending on factors like the nature and duration of the abuse, the relationship with the abuser, the presence of supportive relationships, and access to therapeutic interventions. Recovery and healing are possible with appropriate support and therapy, although the journey can be complex and nonlinear.

It's easy to look at our current behaviors and write them off as being just part of who I am or what I know. It's also easy to blame past abuse and people who hurt us for how we do things today. In the end, it's on us. We choose what we do with it. It's an important step to accept that concept. If we can concede that we can't undo what's done, we can then ask, "What do I want to do about it now?" The next chapter will take the different types of abuse and neglect and explore strategies to heal and grow from them. After all, what doesn't kill you, makes you stronger. We can thank Nietzsche for that one.

Chapter 7

CONTROLLING THE EFFECTS OF ABUSE

*"Healing doesn't mean the damage never existed. It
means the damage no longer controls our lives."*
– Unknown

In my career and in my life, I have heard extraordinary stories from people. The reason I am able to hear the stories is that people were willing to share them. One indicator of people healing from past negative experiences is when they are able to talk about them. Talking about abuse is a method that allows us to take control of it. When we can't, or won't, it usually means that the abuse still has a hold on us. We can't rewrite what has occurred, but we can decide how to write about it now. We've all heard that whatever doesn't destroy us only makes us stronger. By talking about past hurt and learning ways to learn and grow from it, gives us the opportunity to take something we couldn't control and morphing it into something we can.

Healing From Physical Abuse

Healing from physical abuse is a deeply personal process that involves both psychological and physical dimensions. It often requires time, patience, and a multifaceted approach to address the complex effects of trauma. Here are several strategies to consider for psychological healing after experiencing physical abuse:

1. *Acknowledge and Validate Your Experience*

Recognize the Abuse: Acknowledging that you have been a victim of physical abuse is a crucial first step in the healing process. Recognizing the harm done to you allows you to begin understanding its impact on your life.

Validate Your Feelings: It's important to accept and validate all of your feelings related to the abuse–anger, sadness, fear, confusion. These emotions are natural responses to trauma.

2. *Seek Professional Support*

Therapy: A mental health professional specializing in trauma can offer invaluable support. Therapies such as Cognitive Behavioral Therapy (CBT), Eye Movement Desensitization and Reprocessing (EMDR), and trauma-focused cognitive behavioral therapy (TF-CBT) are effective in treating trauma.

Support Groups: Joining a support group for survivors of physical abuse can provide a sense of community and understanding. Sharing your experiences with others who have faced similar challenges can be incredibly validating and empowering.

3. *Develop Healthy Coping Strategies*

Mindfulness and Relaxation Techniques: Practices such as meditation, deep breathing, and yoga can help reduce stress and anxiety, promoting emotional balance. Guided meditation is an extremely valuable tool that can be used anywhere–your home, office, outside, the train, etc. It's as simple as searching for guided meditation on your music app or YouTube and following the instructions.

Physical Activity: Regular physical activity can improve mood and decrease symptoms of depression and anxiety. Find an activity you enjoy and make it a regular part of your routine. I've had some of my best workouts after a situation that has gone poorly. Exercise is one of the best coping skills as it works on so many levels. Exercise is a natural anti-depressant, it helps your body in a number of ways, and makes you stronger mentally and physically.

Creative Expression: Art, writing, music, and other forms of creative expression can be therapeutic outlets for emotions and thoughts related to abuse. Creativity offers numerous psychological benefits and plays a significant role in mental health and cognitive functioning. Creative activities like learning to play a musical instrument, painting, or writing can increase neuroplasticity–the brain's ability to form new neural connections. This enhances the brain's ability to adapt and learn throughout life. Creative thinking encourages looking at situations from multiple perspectives, leading to better problem-solving skills. This kind of thinking can apply to everyday life challenges, promoting more innovative and effective solutions.

Engaging in creative activities can be meditative and relaxing, helping to alleviate stress. Activities such as drawing, gardening, or playing music can provide a break from stressors and allow the mind to reset. Creativity increases levels of dopamine, a neurotransmitter that helps control the brain's reward and pleasure centers. This can boost mood and overall well-being. Creative expression provides an outlet for communicating feelings that might be difficult to express verbally. This can be particularly therapeutic for people dealing with trauma or emotional challenges.

Completing creative projects can boost self-esteem and promote a sense of accomplishment. Overcoming artistic challenges can enhance one's confidence in handling various life situations.

Engaging in creative processes requires flexibility and adaptability, as outcomes often don't match initial expectations. This can enhance one's ability to adapt more readily to changes and setbacks in everyday life.

Many creative activities involve social interactions, whether in classes, workshops, or online communities. These can strengthen social ties and provide emotional support, reducing feelings of isolation. Creative expression offers new ways of communication, which can enhance interpersonal skills and the ability to convey complex emotions and thoughts.

Creative activities can promote a heightened state of awareness, concentration, and focus. The immersive experience of creating can act as a form of mindfulness, keeping the creator fully present in the moment. Arts like writing, painting, and acting encourage reflection on one's life experiences and emotions, providing deeper personal insights and fostering personal growth.

Engaging in creative endeavors can give a sense of purpose and meaning, which is linked to higher life satisfaction and overall mental health. Creativity isn't limited to artistic talents; it involves any process that includes generating new ideas, solving problems, and expressing oneself in unique ways.

4. *Establish Safety and Stability*

Create a Safe Environment: Ensuring your physical safety is paramount. This may involve relocating or seeking assistance from organizations dedicated to helping survivors of abuse.

Build a Support System: Surround yourself with people who support and believe in you. This could include friends, family, therapists, or members of a support group.

Work on Rebuilding Self-Esteem and Trust

Self-Compassion: Be kind and compassionate to yourself. Understand that healing takes time and that it's okay to have setbacks.

Trust Building: Rebuilding trust after abuse is challenging. Start small by setting boundaries and slowly allowing trustworthy people into your life.

Address Trauma in the Body

Somatic Therapies: Techniques such as somatic experiencing can help you reconnect with your body in a healthy way, learning to interpret its signals and respond to stress more effectively.

5. *Educate Yourself*

Understanding Abuse and Its Effects: Learning about the dynamics of abuse and its psychological effects can empower you and help you recognize patterns and triggers.

6. *Consider Forgiveness (if and when you're ready)*

Personal Choice: Forgiveness is a personal choice and process. It is not about excusing the abuser's actions but about letting go of its power over you, for your own peace and healing.

7. *Establish a Routine*

Routine and Structure: Creating a stable routine can provide a sense of normalcy and control over your life.

8. *Focus on the Future*

Goal Setting: Setting personal and professional goals can help shift your focus towards the future and away from your past experiences of abuse.

Healing from physical abuse is a journey, and it's important to proceed at your own pace. There's no one-size-fits-all approach, and what works for one person may not work for another. Remember, seeking professional help is a sign of strength and an important step in the healing process.

Healing From Emotional Abuse

Healing from emotional abuse is a deeply personal and often complex journey that involves acknowledging the abuse, understanding its impact, and taking steps towards recovery and self-care. Here are some steps and strategies that can help in the healing process:

1. *Acknowledge and Accept the Abuse*

Recognize the Abuse: The first step in healing is acknowledging that the abuse occurred and recognizing that it was not your fault. Emotional abuse can be subtle and insidious, making it difficult to identify.

Accept Your Feelings: Allow yourself to feel and express the emotions that arise from the abuse–anger, sadness, betrayal, or fear. These feelings are valid, and acknowledging them is crucial for healing.

2. *Seek Support*

Therapy: Working with a therapist, especially one who specializes in trauma and abuse, can provide you with the tools and strategies to process your experiences and begin to heal. Therapies like Cognitive Behavioral

Therapy (CBT), Eye Movement Desensitization and Reprocessing (EMDR), and trauma-focused therapy can be particularly helpful.

Support Groups: Joining a support group can offer a sense of community and understanding. Sharing experiences with others who have gone through similar situations can reduce feelings of isolation.

3. *Rebuild Self-Esteem and Identity*

Self-Compassion: Emotional abuse often erodes self-esteem. Practice self-compassion and challenge negative self-beliefs by affirming your worth and strengths.

Rediscover Yourself: Abuse can lead to a loss of identity. Spend time rediscovering your interests, values, and goals. Engage in activities that bring you joy and fulfillment.

4. *Establish Boundaries*

Set Healthy Boundaries: Learning to set healthy boundaries is crucial after experiencing abuse. Identify what you are and aren't comfortable within your relationships and communicate these boundaries clearly.

Limit Contact with the Abuser: If possible, limit or eliminate contact with the person who abused you. If you must maintain contact (e.g., in cases of co-parenting), establish strict boundaries and seek legal advice if necessary.

5. *Develop Coping Strategies*

Mindfulness and Relaxation Techniques: Practices such as mindfulness, meditation, and yoga can help regulate emotions and reduce stress.

Healthy Lifestyle Choices: Engage in physical activity, maintain a nutritious diet, and ensure you get enough sleep. Physical well-being significantly impacts emotional health.

6. *Work on Forgiveness (if applicable)*

Personal Forgiveness: For some, forgiveness (which is a personal journey and does not necessitate reconciliation with the abuser) can be a powerful step in healing. It's about letting go of the hold the experience has on you, for your own peace of mind. Forgiveness does not mean the other person was right for what they did, it's about freeing yourself of the weight that many carry unnecessarily. I knew a person who was wrongly convicted and served nine years in jail. Afterward, he saw the person who had set him up. I asked him what he did and he said he walked the other way because "God hates ugly". He went on to say he can't carry hate and be happy, so he doesn't.

It's also important to forgive yourself. Many people carry guilt about abuse. There are many layers to this concept as they may feel they allowed it, or blame themselves for how the other person acted, or let it go on where it affected other people around them. Guilt can be a powerful motivator for change, but it can also be debilitating to the psyche. Self-forgiveness is just as important as forgiving others.

7. *Rebuild Trust in Relationships*
Take It Slow: Rebuilding trust takes time. Start by establishing trust in smaller, less significant relationships and gradually work your way up as you become more comfortable.

Therapy for Relationships: If you're in a relationship, consider couples therapy to work through trust issues and improve communication.

8. *Educate Yourself*
Learn about Emotional Abuse: Understanding the dynamics of emotional abuse can empower you to recognize abusive patterns in the future and avoid them. Naturally, reading this book and utilizing the resources at the end are a natural step in educating yourself.

9. *Create a Positive Environment*
Surround Yourself with Support: Build a support network of friends, family, and community who understand what you've been through and offer positive reinforcement.

Healing from emotional abuse is not linear; there will be ups and downs. Be patient with yourself and recognize each step forward as progress. It's also important to remember that seeking support is a sign of strength and professional help is available.

Healing From Neglect

Healing from neglect, especially if it occurred during critical developmental periods like childhood, requires an understanding of its profound impact on emotional and psychological well-being. Neglect, which may involve the absence of adequate physical, emotional, or social care, can lead to long-term issues with self-esteem, trust, and interpersonal relationships. Here's a guide to the healing process:

1. *Acknowledge the Neglect*

Recognize the Experience: Understanding that you experienced neglect and acknowledging its impact on your life is an essential first step. Often, those who have been neglected might not immediately recognize their experiences as abusive since neglect involves the absence of actions rather than overt behaviors.

Validating Feelings: It's important to acknowledge and validate the feelings that arise from experiences of neglect, which can include feelings of loneliness, unworthiness, or invisibility.

2. *Seek Professional Help*

Therapy: Engaging with a mental health professional with experience in dealing with childhood neglect and its aftermath can be incredibly beneficial. Therapeutic approaches like Cognitive Behavioral Therapy (CBT), Dialectical Behavior Therapy (DBT), and trauma-informed therapy are often used to treat the effects of neglect.

Support Groups: Joining support groups where others share similar backgrounds can help alleviate the sense of isolation and provide peer understanding and support.

3. *Develop Healthy Relationships*

Building Trust: Learning to trust others can be particularly challenging for those who've experienced neglect. Therapy can help in developing strategies to building healthy relationships gradually and setting appropriate boundaries.

Social Skills: Because neglect can impact social development, working on social skills through group therapy or social activities can be beneficial.

4. *Foster Self-Esteem and Self-Worth*

Positive Self-Talk: Changing the narrative about oneself from negative to positive through affirmations and positive self-talk can help in rebuilding self-esteem.

Self-Compassion: Practicing self-compassion involves treating yourself with the same kindness and understanding as you would a friend.

5. *Establish a Routine*

Structured Daily Routine: Creating a predictable daily routine can provide a sense of stability and security that was missing due to neglect.

6. *Engage in Self-Care*

Physical Care: Regular exercise, a nutritious diet, and adequate sleep can improve overall well-being and help stabilize mood.

Emotional Care: Engaging in activities that you enjoy and that make you feel good can help improve your mood and your outlook on life.

7. *Reconnect with Your Body*

Mindfulness and Meditation: These practices can help you reconnect with your body and learn to better understand its signals and needs.

Somatic Therapies: Techniques like yoga or somatic experiencing can be helpful in overcoming the disconnection from one's body that often results from neglect.

8. *Build New Competencies*

Learning New Skills: Taking up hobbies, learning new skills, or engaging in educational activities can boost self-confidence and provide a sense of achievement and purpose.

9. *Create Meaningful Experiences*

Volunteering: Helping others can create a sense of value and purpose, which is often lacking in those who have experienced neglect. Helping others can also take us out of our own pain. People who have experienced neglect often feel bad about what wasn't done for them when they were younger, and it's very cathartic to be able to do for others. I often recommend to patients that they get involved in helping people less fortunate as it genuinely feels good to help others. It's also an opportunity for us to reflect on what we have rather than focusing on what we don't. Another benefit of volunteering is it puts you around people who like to help others, and that's a healthy energy to be around.

10. *Process Past Trauma*

Narrative Therapy: Writing about or otherwise narrating your experiences can help you process and make sense of them. The approach to writing can vary. Some people write about their experiences in order to make sense of them and process them. Others write letters to the people that harmed them. The letters usually aren't sent, but it helps us to put words to what we would like to say to the person. It's less about the other person reading it and more about coming to some level of closure.

One of my preferred approaches to life is focusing on the present and future, which is ironic since this book is about the past. I've always liked the idea that we are writing our own script. My grandmother used to love this idea and wanted me to write a book about that (maybe the next one). In a way, this book would be the prelude to that idea since it positions us to learn what we need to address from the past to make a better present and future. By writing our own script for life, we let go of notions like predetermination and that our past dictates our future.

Healing from neglect is a gradual process that involves addressing the emotional, psychological, and physical repercussions of having fundamental needs unmet. It often requires the support of both professionals and a caring community to fully navigate the journey toward recovery.

Chapter 8

UNDERSTANDING DOMESTIC VIOLENCE

"Domestic violence causes far more pain than the visible marks of bruises and scars. It is devastating to be abused by someone that you love and think loves you in return. It is estimated that approximately 3 million incidents of domestic violence are reported each year in the United States."
– Dianne Feinstein

According to the National Domestic Violence Hotline website:

1. More than 1 in 3 women (35.6%) and more than 1 in 4 men (28.5%) in the U.S. will experience rape, physical violence, and/or stalking by an intimate partner in their lifetime.
2. Nearly 20 people are physically abused by an intimate partner each minute in the U.S. This adds up to more than 10 million women and men experiencing domestic violence each year.
3. 1 in 4 women and 1 in 7 men have experienced severe physical violence by an intimate partner during their lifetime.
4. Intimate partner violence accounts for 15% of all violent crimes.
5. On a typical day, domestic violence hotlines receive more than 20,000 phone calls nationwide.
6. Worldwide, almost one-third (27%) of women aged 15–49 years who have been in a relationship report that they have been

subjected to some form of physical and/or sexual violence by their intimate partner.

7. During their lifetime, 1 in 4 gay men, 1 in 3 bisexual men, and 3 in 10 heterosexual men will experience rape, physical violence, and/or stalking by an intimate partner.

8. Forty-four percent of lesbian women and 61% of bisexual women have experienced rape, physical violence, or stalking by an intimate partner.

9. Nearly 2 in 5 transgender people report experiencing intimate partner violence or other forms of coercive control and/or physical harm.

10. More than half of all cases of domestic violence are never reported to the police.

11. In domestic violence homicides, women are six times more likely to be killed when a gun is in the house.

12. Every year, 1 in 15 children are exposed to intimate partner violence, and 90% of these children are eyewitnesses to this violence.

13. Forty-seven percent of American Indian/Alaska Native women, 45.1% of non-Hispanic Black women, 37.3% of non-Hispanic White women, 34.4% of Hispanic women, and 18.3% of Asian-Pacific Islander women have experienced sexual violence, physical violence, and/or stalking by an intimate partner in their lifetime.

14. Globally, intimate partners are responsible for as many as 38% of all murders of women.

15. Women with disabilities have a 40% greater risk of intimate partner violence, especially severe violence, than women without disabilities.

16. Fifty-three percent of female violence survivors who are still involved with the perpetrator experienced self-blame for causing the violence.

17. Approximately 63% of homeless women have experienced domestic violence in their adult lives.

18. Twenty percent of female high school students report being physically and/or sexually abused by an intimate partner.
19. The lifetime economic cost of intimate partner violence to the U.S. population is estimated to be $3.6 trillion.
20. On average, more than three women and one man are murdered by their intimate partners every day in the U.S.

What Is Domestic Violence?

Domestic violence (DV) is the use of any form of violence by one person to control another, and is used to describe any abuse that occurs in intimate relationships. In the majority of cases of domestic violence, the victims are women. The abuse may continue long after the relationship has ended.

Domestic Violence Against Women

Domestic violence needs to be understood in the context of social inequality, not on the dynamics of individual relationships. Generally, women in a DV situation do not enter into a relationship believing that it will become violent. There are occasions when women may make long-term relationship commitments, believing that a marriage or marriage-like commitment would put a stop to extreme jealousy and possessiveness. There are also occasions when women enter longer-term commitments out of fear.

For many women, physical and sexual violence does not begin until a year or so into a long-term relationship, often during pregnancy. Controlling and dominating behavior prior to long-term commitment is often interpreted as jealousy and sometimes considered a compliment to a woman as a sign of his love for her. Within a relationship, disagreements and arguments do occur. This is normal, and both partners should be able to put forward their different points of view or concerns and discuss them together. It is not normal for one partner to feel threatened, too frightened to argue back, disagree, or express their opinion.

Types of abuse

There are different types of abuse. They are commonly in the areas of fear, intimidation, verbal abuse, emotional abuse, social, economic, sexual, and staking. Fear is a key element in DV and is often the most powerful way a perpetrator controls his victim. Fear can be created by looks, gestures, possession of weapons (even when they may not be used), destruction of property, cruelty to pets—or any behavior which can be used to intimidate and render powerless.

Intimidation includes harassing her at her workplace either by persistent phone calls or text messages, following her to and from work, or loitering near work. It could also include smashing things, destroying her property, putting a fist through the wall, handling of guns or other weapons, intimidating body language (angry looks, raised voice), hostile questioning and reckless driving.

Verbal Abuse: Verbal abuse includes screaming, shouting, put-downs, name-calling, sarcasm and ridicule about beliefs.

Physical Abuse: Physical violence can range from a lack of consideration for physical comfort to permanent damage or death. It could include such behavior as pushing, shoving, hitting, slapping, choking, hair-pulling, punching etc. and may or may not involve the use of weapons. It could also be threats to, or actually destroying prized possessions.

Emotional Abuse: Deliberately undermining confidence, leading her to believe she is insane, stupid, a "bad mother" or useless. This type of abuse humiliates, degrades and demeans the victim. Threats include those to harm them or someone else, threats to take the children, and to commit suicide. Behavior can also be silent and withdrawing.

Social Abuse: This behavior includes isolation from social networks, and verbal or physical abuse in public or in front of friends and family.

Economic Abuse: This results in the victim being financially dependent on her partner by denying access to money, including her own, and demanding that she and the children live on inadequate resources. These can be contributing factors for women becoming trapped in abusive relationships.

Sexual Abuse: Sexual assault is an act of violence, power and control. It can include many behaviors, including forced sexual contact, being forced to perform sexual acts that cause pain or humiliation, forcing her to have sex with others, and causing injury.

Controlling Behaviors: Controlling what she does, who she sees and talks to, where she goes, keeping her from making any friends, talking to her family, or having any money, preventing her from going to work, not allowing her to express her own feelings and thoughts, not allowing her any privacy, forcing her to go without food or water. Not allowing cultural, religious or personal freedom. Controlling behaviors may be linked to unfounded jealousy.

Stalking: Stalking can involve various activities such as loitering, sending persistent telephone calls and mail and being continually watched. To be classified as stalking, more than one type of behavior has to occur or the same behavior has to occur more than once.

Domestic Violence Against Men

Domestic violence against men is a significant issue, though it is often less recognized and reported than violence against women. Men can be victims of various forms of abuse, including physical, emotional, psychological, and sexual abuse. Naturally, there are some similar dynamics, as the overarching theme with domestic violence is about power and control. Below are some key points about domestic violence against men.

Types of Abuse
Physical Abuse: This includes hitting, slapping, punching, kicking, and other forms of physical harm. In my work, I have experienced a number of males who reported that they were struck by their female partners. They didn't hit back and also didn't leave. At times, they did report it, but it wasn't taken seriously. This isn't surprising, as it is difficult for many of us to understand why someone who may not seem physically vulnerable would stay in a situation where they are being hit by their partner and then report that they felt unsafe.

Another common theme in domestic violence cases is dysfunction in the relationship. When domestic violence incidents happen, they are often a culmination of problems. The way I describe it in therapy is that for every line we cross, the next one is that much closer. Healthy relationships are based on agreeing which lines are not to be crossed way before the more explosive lines.

Emotional and Psychological Abuse: This includes verbal abuse, manipulation, threats, and controlling behavior designed to undermine the victim's self-esteem and mental health.

Sexual Abuse: This involves any non-consensual sexual acts or coercion into unwanted sexual activities.

Economic Abuse: This includes controlling a partner's access to financial resources, limiting their ability to work, or stealing their money.

Prevalence and Challenges

Underreporting: Men are less likely to report domestic violence due to societal stigma, shame, fear of not being believed, or not recognizing their experiences as abuse.

Lack of Support Services: There are fewer support services specifically tailored for male victims, such as shelters and counseling services.

Gender Stereotypes: Cultural and societal norms often depict men as strong and self-reliant, making it difficult for male victims to seek help and be taken seriously.

Effects on Male Victims

Emotional and Mental Health Issues: Male victims of domestic violence can experience depression, anxiety, PTSD, and other mental health conditions.

Physical Injuries: Men can sustain injuries from physical abuse, some of which may require medical attention.

Social Isolation: Abusers often isolate their victims from friends and family, leading to loneliness and a lack of support.

Impact on Relationships and Work: Abuse can strain relationships with friends, family, and colleagues, and affect job performance and stability.

Barriers to Seeking Help

Fear of Judgment: Men may fear being judged or ridiculed if they disclose their abuse.

Legal System Challenges: The legal system may not always recognize or respond adequately to male victims of domestic violence.

Lack of Awareness: There is often a lack of awareness among men that they can be victims of domestic violence and that help is available.

Support and Resources

Hotlines and Counseling: There are hotlines and counseling services available specifically for male victims of domestic violence.

Support Groups: Support groups for male victims can provide a sense of community and understanding.

Legal Assistance: Legal aid services can help male victims navigate restraining orders, custody issues, and other legal matters related to their abuse.

Domestic violence against men is a serious issue that requires greater awareness and resources. It's crucial to break the stigma and provide support to all victims of domestic violence, regardless of gender. Recognizing the signs, offering support, and advocating for more resources can help male victims find the help they need to escape abusive situations and begin healing.

Domestic Violence in Same-Sex Relationships

Domestic violence in same-sex relationships is a critical issue that often goes underreported and inadequately addressed due to various societal and systemic factors. Understanding the unique challenges faced by individuals in same-sex relationships is essential for providing appropriate support and interventions. Below are the key aspects of domestic violence in same-sex relationships.

Unique Challenges

Stigma and Discrimination: Same-sex couples may face additional barriers due to societal stigma, homophobia, and discrimination, which can prevent them from seeking help.

Lack of Recognition: Domestic violence in same-sex relationships is often not recognized or taken seriously by authorities and support services, leading to inadequate responses.

Isolation: Victims may feel isolated due to a lack of support from family, friends, or community, especially if their sexual orientation is not accepted.

Outing Threats: Abusers may threaten to "out" their partner's sexual orientation to friends, family, or employers as a form of control and manipulation.

Types of Abuse

Physical Abuse: Includes hitting, slapping, punching, and other forms of physical violence.

Emotional and Psychological Abuse: Includes verbal abuse, threats, manipulation, and controlling behaviors.

Sexual Abuse: Non-consensual sexual acts or coercion into unwanted sexual activities.

Economic Abuse: Controlling financial resources, limiting the victim's ability to work, or stealing money.

Identity Abuse: Using the victim's sexual orientation or gender identity against them, such as ridiculing their identity or threatening to reveal it to others.

Barriers to Seeking Help

Fear of Homophobia: Victims may fear encountering homophobia from service providers, law enforcement, or within their own social circles.

Limited Services: There are fewer support services specifically tailored to the needs of LGBTQ+ individuals, including shelters and counseling services.

Misconceptions: There are misconceptions that domestic violence does not occur in same-sex relationships or that it is less severe, which can minimize the victim's experiences.

Legal and Institutional Barriers: In some regions, legal protections and resources for LGBTQ+ individuals may be lacking or insufficient.

Effects on Victims

Mental Health Issues: Victims may experience depression, anxiety, PTSD, and other mental health conditions.

Physical Injuries: Victims can sustain injuries that require medical attention.

Social Isolation: Abusers often isolate their victims from support networks, leading to loneliness and a lack of support.

Impact on Daily Life: Domestic violence can affect victims' ability to work, maintain relationships, and perform daily activities.

Support and Resources

LGBTQ+ Friendly Services: Providing access to support services that are inclusive and affirming of LGBTQ+ identities, such as shelters, hotlines, and counseling.

Education and Training: Training for service providers and law enforcement on the specific needs and challenges faced by LGBTQ+ victims of domestic violence.

Community Support: Building supportive communities and networks that can provide emotional and practical support to victims.

Legal Assistance: Providing legal support to help victims navigate restraining orders, custody issues, and other legal matters related to their abuse.

Domestic violence in same-sex relationships is a serious issue that requires greater awareness, understanding, and resources. Addressing the unique challenges faced by LGBTQ+ individuals and ensuring that support services are inclusive and accessible is crucial for helping victims escape abusive situations and begin the healing process. By fostering a more inclusive society and providing tailored support, we can work towards eliminating domestic violence in all relationships.

Generational Domestic Violence

Generational domestic violence, also known as intergenerational transmission of violence, refers to the phenomenon where patterns of abusive behavior are passed down from one generation to the next. This cycle can be perpetuated through learned behaviors, psychological effects, and environmental factors. Below are the key aspects of generational domestic violence.

Causes and Contributing Factors

Learned Behavior: Children who grow up in violent households often learn that abuse is a normal way to handle conflicts and exert control.

Trauma and Mental Health: Exposure to domestic violence can lead to trauma and mental health issues, which can affect a person's behavior and relationships in adulthood.

Social and Environmental Factors: Socioeconomic stressors, lack of education, and limited access to support services can contribute to the perpetuation of domestic violence.

Substance Abuse: Alcohol and drug abuse can exacerbate violent tendencies and contribute to the cycle of abuse.

Effects on Children and Future Generations

Emotional and Psychological Impact: Children exposed to domestic violence may experience anxiety, depression, PTSD, and other mental health issues.

Behavioral Problems: These children may exhibit aggression, defiance, and other behavioral issues. They might also struggle with forming healthy relationships.

Academic and Developmental Issues: Chronic stress and trauma can affect cognitive development, leading to difficulties in school and other areas of life.

Perpetuation of Violence: Children who witness or experience domestic violence are at higher risk of becoming abusers or victims in their own adult relationships.

Breaking the Cycle

Education and Awareness: Raising awareness about the impact of domestic violence and educating individuals about healthy relationships can help break the cycle.

Early Intervention: Identifying and providing support to at-risk families can prevent the perpetuation of violence. This includes counseling, social services, and community programs.

Support Services: Access to mental health services, shelters, and legal assistance is crucial for victims and their children.

Positive Role Models: Providing children with positive role models and stable, nurturing environments can help counteract the negative influences of a violent household.

Therapeutic Interventions: Therapy and counseling for both children and adults who have experienced domestic violence can address trauma and teach healthy coping mechanisms.

Role of Society and Community

Community Programs: Community-based programs can provide education, support, and resources to families affected by domestic violence.

Policy and Legislation: Strong legal frameworks and policies that protect victims, hold abusers accountable, and provide resources for recovery are essential.

Public Awareness Campaigns: Campaigns that destigmatize seeking help and promote awareness of domestic violence can encourage more victims to come forward and seek assistance.

Generational domestic violence is a complex issue that requires a multifaceted approach to address effectively. By understanding the causes and impacts, promoting education and awareness, providing support and resources, and implementing strong policies, it is possible to break the cycle of violence and create healthier environments for future generations.

Effects on Children

Domestic violence has profound and long-lasting effects on children. The impact can manifest in various aspects of a child's life, including emotional, behavioral, social, and cognitive domains. Below are some detailed effects.

Emotional Effects

Anxiety and Depression: Children may develop chronic anxiety or depression due to constant exposure to conflict and violence.

Fear and Insecurity: Living in an unpredictable and volatile environment can create a pervasive sense of fear and insecurity.

Low Self-Esteem: Witnessing a parent being abused can lead to feelings of helplessness and worthlessness.

Behavioral Effects

Aggression and Violence: Some children might mimic violent behavior, believing it's an acceptable way to resolve conflicts.

Withdrawal: Others may withdraw from social interactions and activities, preferring to isolate themselves.

Risky Behaviors: Older children might engage in substance abuse, delinquency, or other risky behaviors as coping mechanisms.

Social Effects

Difficulty Forming Relationships: Trust issues and fear of conflict can hinder a child's ability to form healthy relationships.

Social Isolation: Children may avoid social situations due to embarrassment or fear of others discovering their home situation.

Cognitive Effects

Academic Problems: Stress and anxiety can impair concentration and memory, leading to poor academic performance.

Developmental Delays: Chronic stress can affect brain development, leading to delays in cognitive and emotional development.

Long-term Effects

Chronic Health Issues: Long-term exposure to stress can lead to chronic health problems such as heart disease and mental health disorders.

Cycle of Abuse: Children who witness domestic violence are at a higher risk of perpetuating the cycle of abuse, either as victims or perpetrators.

Protective Factors

Supportive Relationships: Strong, positive relationships with non-abusive adults can mitigate some of the negative effects.

Therapeutic Interventions: Counseling and therapy can help children process their experiences and develop healthy coping mechanisms.

Addressing the effects of domestic violence on children requires a multi-faceted approach involving mental health support, legal interventions, and community resources. It's crucial to create a safe and supportive environment to help these children heal and thrive.

Chapter 9

CONTROLLING THE EFFECTS OF DOMESTIC VIOLENCE

"The wounds of the past may scar, but they do not define your future. Embrace the power of healing and rewrite your story."
– Anonymous

I was conducting a group session one Sunday morning and one of my patients came in very upset. He had found out that his 25-year-old daughter was getting physically abused by her boyfriend. He had gone out the night before our meeting to find and confront the boyfriend but was unable to find him. He explained that he was glad that he didn't find him as he would have hurt him, violated his parole, and gone back to jail. Many men would find jail a reasonable price to pay if it meant protecting their daughter. My patient realized that his daughter was dating someone who was similar to him when he was younger and abusive. He said that if he hurt the guy, his daughter would still go back to him or someone like him. He knew the only chance he had of breaking the family pattern was to help his daughter get help and to be there for her. He knew he couldn't do that from jail. Sadly, this story has many layers as it pertains to domestic violence. Let's try to peel some of them back.

Healing from Witnessing Domestic Violence

Healing from witnessing domestic violence, especially as a child, is a challenging and multifaceted process. It requires addressing the emotional, psychological, and sometimes physical impacts of the experience. Below are some steps and strategies to facilitate healing.

Emotional and Psychological Support
Therapy and Counseling: Professional therapy, including individual and group counseling, can provide a safe space to process emotions and experiences. Cognitive behavioral therapy (CBT) and trauma-focused therapy are particularly effective.

Support Groups: Joining support groups for survivors of domestic violence can help individuals feel less isolated and provide a community of people who understand their experiences.

Building a Support Network
Trusted Relationships: Establishing relationships with trusted friends, family members, or mentors who can provide emotional support and a sense of safety.

Community Resources: Utilizing community resources such as local non-profits, religious organizations, and community centers that offer support services for domestic violence survivors.

Developing Coping Strategies
Mindfulness and Relaxation Techniques: Practices such as mindfulness meditation, deep breathing exercises, and yoga can help manage stress and anxiety.

Journaling: Writing about experiences and emotions can be a therapeutic way to process trauma and track progress over time.

Education and Empowerment
Understanding Domestic Violence: Learning about the dynamics and effects of domestic violence can help survivors understand that they are not to blame for what happened.

Life Skills and Education: Pursuing education and developing life skills can empower survivors to build a stable and independent future.

Creating a Safe Environment

Physical Safety: Ensuring physical safety is paramount. This may involve changing living situations, obtaining protective orders, or creating a safety plan.

Healthy Boundaries: Learning to set and maintain healthy boundaries in relationships to prevent future abuse and promote respectful interactions.

Long-Term Healing Strategies

Consistent Therapy: Long-term therapy can help individuals work through deep-seated trauma and develop healthy coping mechanisms.

Holistic Approaches: Integrating holistic approaches such as art therapy, music therapy, and animal-assisted therapy can complement traditional therapeutic methods.

Self-Care and Wellness

Physical Health: Regular exercise, a balanced diet, and adequate sleep are crucial for overall well-being and stress management.

Hobbies and Interests: Engaging in hobbies and activities that bring joy and satisfaction can provide a sense of normalcy and fulfillment.

Building Resilience

Strengthening Self-Esteem: Working on self-esteem and self-worth through positive affirmations and achieving small, manageable goals.

Resilience Training: Learning resilience-building techniques to better handle future stressors and challenges.

Professional and Legal Support

Legal Assistance: Accessing legal support to address any ongoing legal issues related to the domestic violence situation, such as custody arrangements or restraining orders.

Professional Development: Seeking career counseling and professional development opportunities to build financial independence and stability.

Healing from witnessing domestic violence is a journey that requires time, patience, and support. It's important to seek professional help, build a strong support network, and develop healthy coping strategies. With the right resources and support, individuals can overcome the effects of domestic violence and lead fulfilling, healthy lives.

Surviving Domestic Violence

Healing from being a victim of domestic violence is a multifaceted process that involves addressing the physical, emotional, psychological, and social impacts of the abuse. Below are steps and strategies to support the healing journey.

Immediate Steps
Ensure Physical Safety: The first priority is to ensure physical safety. This might involve leaving the abusive environment, seeking shelter, and obtaining legal protection such as restraining orders.

Medical Attention: Address any immediate physical injuries and health concerns by seeking medical attention.

Emotional and Psychological Healing
Therapy and Counseling: Engaging in therapy is crucial. Cognitive behavioral therapy (CBT), trauma-focused therapy, and other forms of counseling can help process and heal from the trauma.

Support Groups: Joining support groups for domestic violence survivors can provide a sense of community and shared experiences, reducing feelings of isolation.

Building a Support Network
Trusted Relationships: Reconnecting or building relationships with trusted friends, family members, or mentors who can provide emotional support and a sense of security.

Community Resources: Utilizing community resources such as non-profits, religious organizations, and community centers that offer support services for survivors.

Developing Coping Strategies

Mindfulness and Relaxation Techniques: Practices such as mindfulness meditation, deep breathing exercises, and yoga can help manage stress and anxiety.

Journaling: Writing about experiences and emotions can be therapeutic and help in processing the trauma.

Education and Empowerment

Understanding Domestic Violence: Learning about the dynamics and effects of domestic violence can help survivors understand that they are not to blame and can empower them to make informed decisions about their future.

Life Skills and Education: Pursuing education and developing life skills can help in building a stable and independent future.

Creating a Safe Environment

Physical Safety: Ensuring ongoing physical safety by possibly changing living situations, obtaining protective orders, or creating a safety plan.

Healthy Boundaries: Learning to set and maintain healthy boundaries in relationships to prevent future abuse and promote respectful interactions.

Long-Term Healing Strategies

Consistent Therapy: Engaging in long-term therapy to address deep-seated trauma and develop healthy coping mechanisms.

Holistic Approaches: Integrating holistic approaches such as art therapy, music therapy, and animal-assisted therapy can complement traditional therapeutic methods.

Self-Care and Wellness

Physical Health: Maintaining regular exercise, a balanced diet, and adequate sleep is crucial for overall well-being and stress management.

Hobbies and Interests: Engaging in hobbies and activities that bring joy and satisfaction can provide a sense of normalcy and fulfillment.

Building Resilience

Strengthening Self-Esteem: Working on self-esteem and self-worth through positive affirmations and achieving small, manageable goals.

Resilience Training: Learning resilience-building techniques to better handle future stressors and challenges. Resilience is the ability to overcome adversity. Naturally, not everyone is resilient, but there are three common factors in those that are. The factors were extrapolated from research on twins. Twin studies have been very helpful for research in psychology as twins have comparable variables. The factors discovered were: a positive peer group, being acknowledged for a talent or skill, and a significant, trusting relationship with an adult.

Professional and Legal Support

Legal Assistance: Accessing legal support to address any ongoing legal issues related to the domestic violence situation, such as custody arrangements, divorce proceedings, or restraining orders.

Career Counseling: Seeking career counseling and professional development opportunities to build financial independence and stability.

Community and Social Involvement

Community Engagement: Getting involved in community activities or advocacy groups can provide a sense of purpose and connection.

Volunteering: Helping others through volunteer work can be empowering and healing.

Personal Development

Educational Pursuits: Enrolling in courses or workshops to learn new skills or further one's education can be empowering.

Setting Goals: Setting and working towards personal goals can provide direction and motivation.

Long-Term Health Management

Regular Health Check-ups: Keeping up with regular medical and mental health check-ups to monitor and maintain overall well-being.

Mental Health Maintenance: Continuing mental health practices, such as therapy, mindfulness, and stress management techniques, to maintain mental health stability.

Healing from being a victim of domestic violence is a gradual and ongoing process. It involves addressing immediate safety needs, seeking professional help, building a supportive network, and developing coping strategies. Empowerment through education, setting healthy boundaries, and engaging in self-care activities are crucial. With the right support and resources, survivors can rebuild their lives, regain their sense of self, and move towards a healthier, more fulfilling future.

Breaking the Cycle

Breaking the cycle of domestic violence is a complex process that involves individuals, communities, and systems working together to address the root causes and provide effective interventions. Below are key strategies and actions that can help in breaking the cycle.

Education and Awareness

Public Awareness Campaigns: Increasing public awareness about domestic violence, its signs, and its effects through media, educational programs, and community events.

School Programs: Implementing programs in schools to teach children about healthy relationships, conflict resolution, and the importance of consent.

Training for Professionals: Providing training for teachers, healthcare providers, law enforcement, and social workers to recognize and respond appropriately to signs of domestic violence.

Support Services for Victims

Hotlines and Crisis Centers: Ensuring that victims have access to confidential hotlines and crisis centers where they can seek immediate help.

Shelters and Safe Housing: Providing safe shelters and transitional housing for victims escaping abusive situations.

Counseling and Therapy: Offering counseling and therapy services to help victims heal from trauma and develop coping strategies.

Legal Assistance: Providing legal support to help victims obtain restraining orders, navigate custody issues, and understand their rights.

Interventions for Abusers

Behavioral Programs: Implementing intervention programs for abusers to address and change their violent behavior.

Counseling and Therapy: Providing individual and group therapy for abusers to help them understand the impact of their actions and develop healthier ways to manage anger and conflict.

Accountability Measures: Ensuring that abusers are held accountable through legal means and community-based interventions.

Community Involvement

Community Support Networks: Building strong community support networks that can provide resources and support to victims and their families.

Mentorship Programs: Creating mentorship programs where survivors and community leaders can support victims and help them rebuild their lives.

Safe Spaces: Establishing safe spaces in communities where victims can seek refuge and support without fear of judgment or retaliation.

Policy and Legislation

Stronger Legal Protections: Advocating for stronger legal protections for victims of domestic violence, including stricter enforcement of restraining orders and harsher penalties for abusers.

Funding for Support Services: Securing funding for domestic violence shelters, hotlines, counseling services, and other support programs.

Collaboration Between Agencies: Encouraging collaboration between law enforcement, social services, healthcare providers, and non-profits to provide a coordinated response to domestic violence.

Prevention and Early Intervention

Risk Assessment Tools: Utilizing risk assessment tools to identify individuals and families at high risk of domestic violence and providing early interventions.

Parenting Programs: Offering parenting programs that teach non-violent discipline methods and promote healthy family dynamics.

Economic Support: Providing economic support and resources to help victims achieve financial independence and reduce the barriers to leaving abusive relationships.

Long-Term Strategies

Education and Empowerment: Empowering victims through education, job training, and support to rebuild their lives and gain independence.

Cultural Change: Promoting cultural change that challenges norms and behaviors that condone or perpetuate domestic violence.

Research and Evaluation: Conducting research to understand the root causes of domestic violence and evaluating the effectiveness of interventions to improve support services and policies.

Breaking the cycle of domestic violence requires a comprehensive approach that involves education, support services, community involvement, policy changes, and long-term strategies. By addressing the issue at multiple levels and providing coordinated support, it is possible to create a safer environment for victims and prevent future generations from experiencing domestic violence.

For those Who Have Been the Domestic Abuser

Changing the behavior of a domestic batterer is a complex process that requires a combination of personal commitment, professional intervention, and supportive environments. Below are key steps and strategies that can help a domestic batterer change.

Acknowledgment and Accountability

Acknowledging the Problem: The batterer must recognize and admit that their behavior is abusive and harmful. This is the first and most crucial step toward change.

Taking Responsibility: They need to take full responsibility for their actions without blaming the victim or external circumstances.

Professional Intervention

Therapy and Counseling: Engaging in individual therapy with a professional who specializes in domestic violence can help address underlying issues such as anger management, emotional regulation, and trauma.

Batterer Intervention Programs (BIPs): Participating in a structured program specifically designed for domestic batterers can provide education about the dynamics of abuse, teach non-violent conflict resolution skills, and promote behavioral change.

Education and Awareness

Understanding Abuse: Learning about the cycle of abuse, the impact of actions on victims, and the long-term consequences of domestic violence can motivate change.

Developing Empathy: Through therapy and education, batterers can develop empathy for their victims, understanding the pain and suffering they have caused.

Building Healthy Relationship Skills

Communication Skills: Learning effective communication skills to express feelings and resolve conflicts without resorting to violence or manipulation.

Healthy Boundaries: Understanding and respecting personal boundaries in relationships.

Support Systems
Support Groups: Joining support groups for individuals seeking to change abusive behavior can provide a sense of community and accountability.

Positive Role Models: Engaging with mentors or peers who model healthy, non-violent behaviors in relationships.

Addressing Underlying Issues
Substance Abuse Treatment: If substance abuse is a contributing factor, seeking treatment for addiction is essential.

Mental Health Support: Addressing any co-occurring mental health issues, such as depression, anxiety, or trauma, that may be influencing abusive behavior.

Long-Term Commitment
Consistent Effort: Changing abusive behavior requires ongoing effort and commitment. Regular participation in therapy and intervention programs is necessary.

Monitoring and Self-Reflection: Continually monitoring behavior and reflecting on actions to ensure non-violent and respectful interactions.

Legal and Social Consequences
Understanding Legal Implications: Recognizing the legal consequences of domestic violence can serve as a deterrent to future abusive behavior.

Facing Consequences: Accepting any legal or social consequences of actions, which can reinforce the seriousness of a person's behavior and the need for change.

Family and Relationship Dynamics
Involving Family: In some cases, involving family members in the healing and accountability process can be beneficial, provided it is safe and appropriate.

Rebuilding Trust: Working on rebuilding trust with an abuser's partner and family, which involves demonstrating consistent, non-violent behavior over time.

Changing the behavior of a domestic batterer is challenging but possible with the right support and commitment. It involves a combination of acknowledging the problem, seeking professional help, learning new skills, and maintaining a long-term commitment to non-violence and healthy relationships. Through these efforts, it is possible for a domestic batterer to change and build a healthier, non-violent future.

Stopping Verbal Abuse in Relationships

Sadly, verbal abuse is very common in most relationships and could be a precursor to domestic violence. When it comes to how people interact with each other, every line one crosses brings them closer to the next line. This can lead to an escalation (negatively) in how two people that love each other treat each other more and more hurtfully. Stopping verbal abuse in relationships involves both partners committing to healthy communication, respect, and accountability. Here are some strategies to help stop verbal abuse. Keep in mind, in some relationships, the role of abuser and victim may switch depending on the situation, so both people need to adhere to the concepts discussed.

For the Abuser

Acknowledge the Behavior: Recognize and admit that verbal abuse is happening and that it is harmful.

Seek Professional Help: Engage in therapy or counseling to understand the roots of abusive behavior and learn healthier ways to communicate.

Learn Communication Skills: Develop skills to express emotions and resolve conflicts without resorting to verbal abuse. Techniques like "I" statements and active listening can be helpful.

Practice Self-Control: Work on managing anger and frustration. Techniques such as deep breathing, counting to ten, or taking a time-out can prevent outbursts.

Empathy Development: Try to understand the impact of your words on your partner. Building empathy can reduce the likelihood of verbal abuse.

Apologize and Make Amends: When verbal abuse occurs, sincerely apologize and take steps to make amends. This shows a commitment to change.

For the Victim

Set Clear Boundaries: Clearly communicate that verbal abuse is unacceptable. Define what constitutes verbal abuse and explain the boundaries that should not be crossed.

Seek Support: Engage in therapy or counseling to build self-esteem, develop coping strategies, and get support for dealing with the abuse.

Develop a Safety Plan: If the verbal abuse escalates to physical abuse or you feel unsafe, have a plan in place for leaving the situation and seeking help.

Assertive Communication: Practice assertive communication to express your feelings and needs without being aggressive or passive.

Document the Abuse: Keep a record of abusive incidents. This can be useful for therapeutic purposes and, if necessary, legal action.

For Both Partners

Couples Therapy: Engage in couples therapy to work on communication skills, conflict resolution, and rebuilding trust.

Commit to Change: Both partners need to commit to changing the dynamic of the relationship and creating a healthier environment.

Educate Yourselves: Learn about the dynamics of verbal abuse and healthy communication techniques through books, workshops, or online resources.

Practice Healthy Communication: Regularly practice healthy communication techniques such as active listening, empathy, and respectful dialogue.

Establish Consequences: Agree on consequences for abusive behavior. This could include taking a break from the conversation, seeking immediate counseling, or other measures.

Focus on Positive Interaction: Make a conscious effort to engage in positive interactions, express appreciation, and build a supportive relationship.

Preventive Measures

Stress Management: Both partners should develop and use stress management techniques to reduce tension and prevent abusive outbursts.

Regular Check-ins: Have regular check-ins to discuss the relationship, address any concerns, and ensure both partners feel heard and respected.

Healthy Lifestyle: Maintain a healthy lifestyle, including regular exercise, adequate sleep, and a balanced diet, to support overall well-being and emotional stability.

Stopping verbal abuse in relationships requires a commitment to change, professional support, and the development of healthy communication skills. Both partners must work together to create a respectful and supportive environment. With dedication and effort, it is possible to stop verbal abuse and build a healthier, more positive relationship.

When it comes to domestic violence, there are many layers due to generational and experiential exposure and trauma. For some, it's in the past, and for others, it's very much in the present. Hopefully, the past two chapters have helped you understand how many people have experienced and been impacted by seeing or surviving domestic violence. Sadly, it's much more common than many realize. Luckily, there are many great resources and services for getting out of dangerous relationships or healing from negative situations. If you've been impacted by domestic violence, I can't implore you enough to do the work detailed in these chapters before engaging in another intimate relationship.

You may be asking, "When is someone ready for the next relationship?" When it comes to relationships after domestic violence, it's important to articulate what happened before and be able to answer these questions: What did I learn about the impact on me? What did I work on and change so that I don't go into a similar dynamic again? What do I want to look for (and avoid) in a romantic partner?

Chapter 10

UNDERSTANDING SEXUAL ABUSE

"Overcoming abuse doesn't just happen, it takes positive steps every day. Let today be the day you start to move forward."
-Assunta Harris

Sexual abuse is one of the most difficult topics to make sense of. How can an adult, or someone close to adulthood, sexually hurt a child? This is a topic we are all aware of, are unable to make sense of, yet it happens to one out of every four females and one out of every six males by the time they turn eighteen. It's possible that those numbers are improving but difficult to know the actual extent. It's also relevant to note that a third of those offenses are committed by someone who is also under the age of eighteen. Either way, it impacts a lot more people than the average person realizes.

According to the Indiana Center for Prevention of Youth Abuse and Suicide:

1. 1 in 4 girls and 1 in 6 boys are sexually abused before the age of 18.
2. 1 in 5 children are solicited sexually on the Internet.
3. Nearly 70% of all reported sexual assaults (including assaults on adults) occur to children ages 17 and under.
4. The median age for reported sexual abuse is 9 years old.

5. More than 20% of children are sexually abused before the age of 8.
6. Nearly 50% of all victims of forcible sodomy, sexual assault with an object, and forcible fondling are children under 12.
7. Many child victims may never disclose their abuse.
8. The way a victim's family responds to abuse plays an important role in how the incident affects the victim.
9. 30-40% of victims are abused by a family member.
10. As many as 50% of victims are abused by someone outside of the family whom they know and trust.
11. Fewer than 10% of victims are abused by strangers.
12. Approximately 40% are abused by older or larger children whom they know.
13. Of those children who are abused by adolescents, 50% are under 12 years of age.
14. People who abuse children look and act just like everyone else.
15. Young girls who are sexually abused are more likely to develop eating disorders as adolescents.
16. Victims of child sexual abuse are more likely to experience major depressive disorder as adults.
17. Evidence that a child has been sexually abused is not always obvious, and many children do not report that they have been abused.

The Box

The only comforting concept with the sobering statistics is that victims are not alone. Sadly, it seems that one of the common effects of sexual abuse is the feeling of isolation and that no one else would understand. Years ago, I had a patient describe this experience in a poem he entitled, the box. With his permission, here it is:

"In this box there is a cold empty feeling of helplessness, of loneliness where I look for comfort but I cannot find it so

I am left alone with no one to talk to, no one to share my problems with.

I can see outside of this box that I am in, through a small window in the door, and I see a dim narrow hallway, not knowing what to expect, and I can hear the voice of the one who frightens me through that small window.

There is also a small window that glances outside, yet I am on the inside and I can hear people, and I see them, but I feel that they do not see or hear me. I want to cry out to be heard, and yet nothing comes out, for fear overtakes me.

The air from the large window is fresh and clean. I hear the birds singing, and I see the squirrels playing, I feel the heat of the sun upon my face. I hear laughter in the backyard, "as though I should be there" as though nothing was wrong with my life, and not here in the box.

The air from the small window is stale, and it is cold, it is dark and it frightens me so. Oh there is something wrong with this, I feel as though something is not right. The discomfort, the loneliness, and the helplessness of this box that I am in.

Does anyone care for me? Does anyone feel my pain? Can anyone hear me cry out? Oh, and the loneliness within, but who can I trust anymore to make these problems go away?

Where is the one that I trust, the one that I love, the one that I looked up to all the days of my life?

I see him through that small window, for it was he who put me into this box that I cannot get out of on my own. Oh how I want to cry out to someone or anyone, but yet I am afraid to. I am afraid of the one who put me in this box.

He has power over me, he has control, he has authority. He is not the same person that I had known at one time.

He was my provider, my teacher, my comforter, my caretaker, my father figure, my guardian, my problem solver, and my friend, he is the one who I trusted, the one who I loved, the one who I looked up to, the one of whom I am now afraid of, for he has built within me this box that I now live in.

The small window that I have looked through, I am looking directly at my fears, the one who had built this box, and I cannot get away for I am trapped from within.

The large window I have looked through, I am looking at what should be the reality of my life, a normal, natural, healthy childhood.

I look around and I see other people playing and smiling and I am with them also playing and smiling (but only on the outside) whereas I do not feel as though I fit in anymore, as if am in a trance, a trance of discomfort, confusion, shame and guilt, I do not feel the joy that they feel within, I feel the hurt, the anger and the misguidance.

If I am outside laughing and playing, or at school, I am still in this box, and the house that I live in, is it not my home? For it is part of this box and where this box was built, it is where my dreams bring me back to, with the memories of this box.

Even now, if I am with my friends or in school, at the park, on the beach, at the mall or with my family, no matter where I go, or who I am with, from now until the ages carry me away, there is no one that I feel I can trust and I fear yet, that I will always be and still am in this box that was built for me within, a box that no one would understand.

I find myself in a box where there are four walls around me, and yet a part of me is trapped in another box, maybe, just maybe the same one that I had built for someone."

Why?

As professionals, we have some insight into the unfathomable, but it still defies logic. In fact, it is often based on illogic in the form of cognitive distortions. Cognitive distortions are the product of changing ones' thoughts to fit the situation. In short, we do what we do because we want to do it. In order to do things that we know are legally or morally wrong, we give ourselves permission in the form of the distortions. So basically, someone who sexually abuses a child minimizes or ignores the negative impact on the child in order to get their needs met. In trying to understand the actual process, David Finkelhor developed the Four Preconditions Model to offending.

The motivation to sexually abuse is the first and most critical condition. This is the core of where the sexual interest in a child originates. According to Finkelhor, a number of factors can contribute to this interest. The primary factor is emotional congruence, where the offender's emotional age is closer to that of a child. This can be caused by arrested emotional development, a need to feel powerful and controlling, re-enactment of childhood trauma to undo the hurt, and a narcissistic identification with the self as a young child.

Arrested emotional development can be caused by a number of factors. One factor is an experience that impacted one's emotional development. This can include abuse or neglect during childhood that could have prevented the child from progressing through developmental stages. Arrested emotional development could also be caused by an experience that disrupts a child's development, such as divorce or moving. Sexual offenders with young ages of preference are often psychologically stuck near their age of preference. If this conflict is not resolved, it is difficult for the offender to progress past their age of interest.

At times, arrested emotional development can be the result of regression. An adult offender may have progressed within normal range through their developmental milestones and experienced a traumatic event as an adult. This can result in a regression in their emotional development. "Oscar's" wife left him for another woman when he was 48. He began socializing with his teenaged sons and their friends. He had sex with at least one of their female friends when she was sixteen and was convicted of rape. It appeared his emotional development regressed to that of his sixteen-year-old son as a result of the failure of his marriage.

Another component to the motivation is having deviant sexual arousal. Factors that can contribute to this may be childhood sexual experiences that were traumatic or strongly conditioning, fantasies and masturbation to deviant arousal, the modeling of sexual interest in children by someone else, such as child pornography, or a mis-attribution of arousal cues (Finkelhor, 1984). Some pedophiles report that they did not have any traumatic experiences during childhood. They report that they were just born with a sexual interest in children.

The last part of the motivation is a result of blockage. This can occur from a fear of adult relationships, traumatic sexual experiences with adults, inadequate social skills, and relationship problems. The psychology of the motivation is the causal component of sexual abuse. Even though the motivation to sexually abuse has common themes, prevention and treatment must begin and end with this condition.

The second precondition is overcoming internal inhibitors. This is the stage where the person knows what they want to do is wrong but gives themselves permission to act on it. There are a number of factors that lead to that permission. They include alcohol or drug use, impulse disorders, failure of incest inhibitions, denial and minimization of harm to the child, a lack of empathy for victims, and cognitive distortions. While preconditions one and two account for the abuser's behavior, preconditions three and four consider the environment outside the abuser and child, which controls whether and whom he abuses.

The potential abuser must overcome external obstacles and inhibitions prior to sexual abuse. External inhibitors that may restrain the abuser's action include family composition, neighbors, peers and societal sanctions, as well as the level of supervision a child receives. Although a child cannot be supervised twenty-four hours per day, lack of supervision has been found to be a contributing factor to sexual abuse, as has physical proximity and opportunity. External inhibitors are easily overcome if the potential abuser is left alone with an unsupervised child.

In order to facilitate this, an offender will look for or manipulate a caregiver who is absent or ill, not close or protective of the child, is dominated and/or abused by the offender, an isolated family, an unsupervised child, and allows unusual sleeping habits. Other high-risk situations include a parent who has a history of sexual abuse and single parent homes. This leads into the fourth precondition, which is overcoming child resistance to being sexually abused.

This capacity to resist may operate in a very subtle way and does not necessarily involve overt protestations. Abusers may sense which children are good potential targets and can be intimidated or co-coerced to keep a secret or otherwise manipulated. Abusers report that they can almost instinctively pick out a vulnerable child on whom to focus their sexual attentions, while ignoring those who might resist. Frequently, these children may be unaware that they are being sexually approached and have little or no capacity to resist. Some of the risk factors that inhibit the capacity to resist include emotional insecurity and deprivation, a child who lacks knowledge about appropriate sexual behavior, a situation of unusual trust between a child and offender, and coercion and grooming of a child.

Knowing which factors make children vulnerable to abuse is essential in formulating prevention programs. It is important to isolate behaviors that constitute a risk and emphasize those that enhance resistance or avoidance that can empower children to protect themselves. This is not to say that children who are not vulnerable are not abused. Many children may be forced or coerced despite displaying resistance and avoidance behaviors. Some instances of abuse are the result of force, threat or violence, and no matter how much resistance the child displays, the child is unable to prevent the abuse.

Precondition four has three possible outcomes. The first is that the child may resist by overtly saying no and running away, or covertly by displaying a confident and assertive manner that conveys strong messages to the abuser not to try for fear of detection or exposure. The second is that the child may resist but still be abused through force or violence. The third is that a child may resist but be overcome through coercion.

The four pre-conditions for sexual abuse come into play in a logical sequence. The abuser must firstly have the motivation and be able to overcome any internal inhibitions. When these have been overcome, the potential abuser then overcomes external inhibitors and finally the resistance of the child .

Generational Sexual Abuse

Generational sexual abuse refers to the pattern of sexual abuse that is passed down from one generation to the next within a family. This cycle can be perpetuated by various factors, including learned behaviors, unresolved trauma, and dysfunctional family dynamics. Addressing generational sexual abuse requires understanding its causes, effects, and strategies for breaking the cycle.

Causes and Contributing Factors
Learned Behavior: Children who grow up in environments where sexual abuse occurs may come to see such behavior as normal or acceptable, leading them to perpetuate the abuse in their own adult relationships.

Unresolved Trauma: Victims of sexual abuse may carry unresolved trauma into adulthood, which can affect their behavior and relationships. Without proper intervention, they might unintentionally continue the cycle of abuse.

Dysfunctional Family Dynamics: Families with histories of substance abuse, mental health issues, or domestic violence may create environments where sexual abuse is more likely to occur.

Lack of Education and Awareness: A lack of understanding about healthy sexual boundaries and the impact of abuse can contribute to the perpetuation of abuse.

Effects on Victims

Psychological Impact: Victims of generational sexual abuse often experience severe psychological effects, including PTSD, anxiety, depression, and dissociative disorders.

Behavioral Issues: Victims may exhibit self-destructive behaviors, substance abuse, aggression, and difficulties in forming healthy relationships.

Physical Health Problems: Chronic health issues such as gastrointestinal disorders, headaches, and reproductive health problems can result from sexual abuse.

Interpersonal Relationships: Trust issues, intimacy problems, and difficulties in establishing healthy boundaries are common among victims.

Poly-victimization

Poly-victimization refers to experiencing multiple types of victimization, such as sexual abuse, physical abuse, bullying, and domestic violence, often occurring simultaneously or sequentially. This concept emphasizes the cumulative impact of various forms of victimization on an individual's mental, emotional, and physical well-being. Understanding poly-victimization is crucial for providing comprehensive support and interventions for those affected.

Characteristics of Poly-victimization

Multiple Victimization Types: Individuals experience different forms of abuse or victimization, such as sexual abuse, physical assault, emotional abuse, neglect, and witnessing domestic violence.

Cumulative Impact: The effects of poly-victimization are often more severe than those of a single type of victimization, due to the cumulative stress and trauma.

Risk Factors

Family Environment: Dysfunctional family dynamics, including domestic violence, substance abuse, and mental health issues, can increase the risk of poly-victimization.

Community Factors: Living in high-crime areas or communities with limited social support and resources can elevate the risk.

Individual Factors: Certain individual characteristics such as disabilities, social isolation, and previous victimization experiences can make a person more vulnerable to multiple forms of victimization.

Effects of Poly-victimization

Mental Health Issues: Poly-victimized individuals are at a higher risk of developing mental health problems such as depression, anxiety, PTSD, and suicidal ideation.

Behavioral Problems: Increased likelihood of engaging in risky behaviors, substance abuse, aggression, and self-harm.

Physical Health Problems: Chronic health conditions, somatic complaints, and increased susceptibility to illnesses due to prolonged stress.

Academic and Social Impact: Difficulties in school, lower academic achievement, and problems forming and maintaining healthy relationships.

Identifying Poly-victimization

Comprehensive Assessment: Conduct thorough assessments that explore various types of victimization experiences rather than focusing on a single incident.

Screening Tools: Validated screening tools designed to identify multiple forms of victimization in children and adults are available.

Intervention Strategies for Polyvictimization

Integrated Services: Provide integrated and multidisciplinary services that address all types of victimization and their combined effects.

Therapeutic Support: Engage in trauma-informed therapy such as Cognitive Behavioral Therapy (CBT), trauma-focused CBT, and EMDR to help individuals process and heal from multiple traumas.

Support Systems: Establish strong support networks, including family, friends, and community resources, to provide emotional and practical support.

Education and Empowerment: Educate victims about polyvictimization and empower them with coping strategies and resources to prevent further victimization.

Prevention Programs: Implement prevention programs that focus on reducing risk factors, such as improving family dynamics, enhancing community safety, and providing education on healthy relationships.

Role of Professionals

Training and Awareness: Train professionals, including educators, healthcare providers, social workers, and law enforcement, to recognize signs of polyvictimization and respond appropriately.

Holistic Approach: Adopt a holistic approach that considers the interconnectedness of different victimization experiences and addresses the overall well-being of the individual.

Advocacy: Advocate for policies and practices that protect individuals from multiple forms of victimization and provide adequate support for survivors.

Polyvictimization highlights the complex and multifaceted nature of victimization experiences. Addressing this issue requires a comprehensive, integrated approach that considers the cumulative impact of multiple traumas. By providing holistic support, fostering strong support networks, and implementing effective prevention strategies, it is possible to help individuals heal and break the cycle of victimization.

Child-on-Child Sexual Abuse

As mentioned earlier, approximately one third of child sexual abuse is perpetrated by someone under the age of eighteen. Child-on-child sexual abuse, also known as peer-on-peer sexual abuse, involves one child engaging in sexual activities with another child without consent, through coercion, or when there is a significant age or developmental difference. This form of abuse is a serious issue that can have long-lasting effects on both the victim and the perpetrator. Addressing it requires understanding its dynamics, identifying the signs, and implementing effective interventions.

Characteristics and Risk Factors

Age and Developmental Differences: The abuse often involves an age or developmental difference where the older or more developed child uses their power to exploit the younger or less developed child.

Power Imbalance: Factors such as physical strength, intellectual ability, or social status can create a power imbalance that facilitates abuse.

Exposure to Sexual Content: Children who have been exposed to sexual content or have experienced abuse themselves are at higher risk of engaging in abusive behaviors.

Lack of Supervision: Inadequate supervision and boundaries can create opportunities for abuse to occur.

Trauma History: Children who have experienced trauma or neglect may act out sexually as a way of coping with their own experiences.

Signs and Symptoms

Behavioral Changes: Sudden changes in behavior, such as aggression, withdrawal, anxiety, or depression.

Sexualized Behavior: Age-inappropriate sexual behavior or knowledge.

Physical Signs: Unexplained injuries, bruises, or infections in the genital area.

Emotional Distress: Increased fear, nightmares, or difficulty sleeping.

Relationship Issues: Problems with peer relationships, such as difficulty making friends or increased conflicts.

Interventions and Responses

Immediate Safety: Ensure the immediate safety of the victim by separating them from the perpetrator and providing a safe environment.

Professional Assessment: Engage professionals to assess the situation comprehensively, including child protective services, mental health professionals, and law enforcement if necessary.

Therapeutic Support for Victims: Provide trauma-informed therapy for the victim to help them process their experiences and heal.

Intervention for Perpetrators: Offer therapeutic interventions for the child who perpetrated the abuse to address underlying issues and prevent future harmful behavior.

Family Support: Engage with the families of both the victim and the perpetrator to provide education, support, and resources.

Education and Prevention: Implement educational programs that teach children about healthy boundaries, consent, and respect for others. These programs should also educate parents and caregivers about recognizing signs of abuse and promoting safe environments.

Supervision and Monitoring: Increase supervision and establish clear boundaries to prevent opportunities for abuse.

School and Community Involvement: Work with schools and community organizations to create safe environments and establish protocols for responding to child-on-child sexual abuse.

Long-Term Strategies

Continued Therapy: Both victims and perpetrators may need ongoing therapeutic support to address the long-term impacts of the abuse.

Support Networks: Building strong support networks for children can help them feel safe and supported as they recover.

Policy and Advocacy: Advocate for policies and practices that protect children from abuse, ensure proper training for professionals, and provide adequate resources for prevention and intervention.

Research and Evaluation: Conduct research to better understand the dynamics of child-on-child sexual abuse and evaluate the effectiveness of intervention programs.

Child-on-child sexual abuse is a serious issue that requires a comprehensive and sensitive approach to address effectively. By ensuring immediate safety, providing therapeutic support, increasing education and prevention efforts, and advocating for strong policies, it is possible to help both victims and perpetrators heal and prevent future abuse. Collaboration among families, professionals, and communities is essential to create safe and supportive environments for all children.

The Effect

One of the early assessment and treatment tools used by many professionals is the Traumagenic Dynamics Model, which was developed by Finkelhor and Browne. This model helps identify where the trauma psychologically occurred for the child victim. The model consists of four broad areas. The first is traumatic sexualization. Traumatic sexualization refers to a process in which a child's sexuality (including both sexual feelings and sexual attitudes) is shaped in a developmentally inappropriate and interpersonally dysfunctional fashion as a result of the sexual abuse. This can happen in a variety of ways in the course of the abuse.

Traumatic sexualization can occur when a child is repeatedly rewarded by an offender for sexual behavior that is inappropriate to his or her level of development. It occurs through the exchange of affection, attention, privileges, and gifts for sexual behavior, so that a child learns sexual behavior as a strategy for manipulating others to get his or her other developmentally appropriate needs met. It occurs when certain parts of a child's anatomy are fetishized and given distorted importance and meaning. It occurs through the misconceptions and confusions about sexual behavior and sexual morality that are transmitted to the child from the offender. It also occurs when very frightening memories and events become associated in the child's mind with sexual activity.

Powerlessness occurs in sexual abuse when a child's territory and body space are repeatedly invaded against the child's will. This is exacerbated by whatever coercion and manipulation the offender may impose as part of the abuse process. Powerlessness is then reinforced when a child sees his or her attempts to halt the abuse frustrated. It is increased when the child feels fear, when he or she is unable to make adults understand or believe what is happening, or when he or she realizes how conditions of dependency have him or her trapped in the situation.

Betrayal refers to the dynamic in which children discover that someone on whom they are vitally dependent has caused them harm. Stigmatization refers to the negative connotations communicated to the child about the experiences and that then become incorporated into the child's self-image. Even though all four dynamics are significant to understanding and treating victims, traumatic sexualization seems to be the most linked to subsequent sexual abuse.

Now that we've increased our understanding of where something like sexual abuse comes from, let's work on taking control back by figuring out how to overcome it. Remember, none of this is okay, even though it happens so much more than people realize. The themes of healing and forgiveness are for the purpose of empowering yourself to choose the impact rather than still being controlled by it.

Chapter 11

CONTROLLING THE EFFECTS
OF SEXUAL ABUSE

*"If someone would have talked in school about safe touch and
unsafe touch, I believe I would have spoken up as a child and
not been victimized over and over again for years, but that
day never came, which is why my mission now is to protect
children from the childhood I could not be protected from."*
– Erin Merryn, An Unimaginable Act: Overcoming
and Preventing Child Abuse Through Erin's Law

Healing and Breaking the Cycle of Sexual Abuse

Therapy and Counseling: Engaging in therapy, both individually and
as a family, is crucial for addressing trauma and dysfunctional patterns.
Therapies such as trauma-focused cognitive behavioral therapy (TF-
CBT) and family therapy can be effective.

Education and Awareness: Providing education about the effects
of sexual abuse and teaching healthy boundaries and relationships can
help prevent the cycle from continuing.

Support Networks: Building strong support networks, including
trusted friends, family members, and support groups, can provide
victims and survivors with emotional and practical support.

Early Intervention: Identifying and addressing signs of abuse early can prevent further harm and break the cycle. This involves training educators, healthcare providers, and community members to recognize and report abuse.

Legal and Protective Measures: Ensuring that victims have access to legal protections and that perpetrators are held accountable can provide safety and justice. This might include restraining orders, child protective services, and criminal prosecution.

Community Programs: Implementing community-based programs that offer support, education, and resources for families affected by generational sexual abuse can help address the issue at a broader level.

Promoting Healthy Relationships: Encouraging and modeling healthy relationship behaviors within families and communities can help break the cycle of abuse.

Role of Society and Community

Awareness Campaigns: Public awareness campaigns can educate communities about the signs of sexual abuse and the importance of reporting it.

Access to Resources: Ensuring that victims have access to resources such as hotlines, shelters, and counseling services is vital for their recovery and safety.

Policy and Legislation: Advocating for strong policies and legislation that protect victims and support their recovery can help prevent generational abuse. This includes funding for victim services and mandatory reporting laws.

Generational sexual abuse is a complex and deeply ingrained issue that requires a multifaceted approach to address effectively. By understanding the causes and effects, providing support and education, and promoting healthy relationships, it is possible to break the cycle of abuse and create a safer, healthier future for all generations. Collaboration between individuals, families, communities, and policymakers is essential to create lasting change.

Confronting Your Abuser

Sadly, 30%–40% of sexual abuse is committed by family members and a larger percentage is committed by someone the victim knows. This means that many victims will have to encounter their offenders for various reasons in their lives. As this book suggests, it's possible to get past sexual abuse and put you in control (it's in the title). In some situations, it's also possible to have safe relationships with the people who have hurt you. Many people have relationships with their abusers without any treatment or clinical intervention. It is less likely that this occurs in a healthy way or with any significant closure.

The ideal scenario is that the person who has been hurt went to therapy and worked on their own healing. Even more ideal, is that the abuser also had successful treatment and is prepared for the clarification session. Some literature calls these meetings apology sessions. I am biased against this concept as an apology often suggests an expectation of forgiveness. In these cases, the victim often feels a pressure to forgive to avoid hurting the abuser's feelings. It's a strange phenomenon, but very common. Apologies and forgiveness are common in the conversation, but should only be if it's helpful to the victim, not based on what the abuser needs. This is because abuse is caused by the abuser getting their needs met at the expense of the victim, and this shouldn't be reflected in therapeutic sessions.

A clarification session begins with the abuser taking full responsibility for the abuse, conveying empathy and insight, and fielding questions and feelings from the person they hurt. Part of the session involves the victim being able to say what they need to feel safe and comfortable moving forward, and the abuser being able to contract to those needs. This is the ideal scenario when continued contact is likely to occur. It should also be done with a clinician trained in this area. Unfortunately, it doesn't always work this way.

I was working with someone, Sam, who had been sexually abused by his grandfather when he was a child. As an adult, it came up in treatment, and he worked on his trauma as best he could. He was still close with his grandmother and would call her once a week. His grandfather would often answer the phone. Sam was used to acting like everything was okay and would have small talk with his grandfather long enough to get his grandmother on the phone. His grandparents lived in a different state and he hadn't seen them in years. In treatment, he worked on confronting his grandfather in terms of what he wanted to accomplish and how to get there.

Sam came in to the office one day and was visibly upset. He explained that he had spoken to his grandfather about the abuse and that his grandfather was dismissive. He basically said that Sam is fine and that this was just psychobabble. He ended the conversation by saying he'll think about what they talked about. Sam saw this as a failure since he didn't get the response he wanted. Remember, needs and wants are different.

He wanted to hear certain things from his grandfather, but he didn't need to. If we base the success of our actions on the behaviors of others, we are powerless. The power was in the confrontation. Sam didn't have to pretend everything was okay to the person who abused him. He was able to assert himself and say he's not okay with acting like nothing ever happened. It would have been great if the grandfather was apologetic and wanted to work on the issue, but he clearly never worked on his issues to be able to have that conversation.

So, what happens next? Should Sam still call grandma? Some would say no, since she seems alright with what happened. When all is said and done, it's up to what Sam thinks. He had forgiven his grandmother years before, as he didn't blame her for not stepping in or defending him and felt bad for her. You could argue whether that's healthy or not, but Sam was at peace with it. At the very least, he confronted his grandfather and had less contact with him, since he still wasn't being treated right. Overall, that's a win for Sam.

So, who should and who shouldn't confront their abuser? It's a complicated question and best answered with a therapist who is versed in this area. At the very least, no one should have to be around someone who has hurt them without some clinical work and safety plan. Most sexual abuse isn't reported, so it's less likely that effective healing has taken place.

Some people feel it's not needed since the abuse may have happened years ago. If that's the case, go back to chapter one and start reading again. It's natural to want to avoid dealing with past abuse, but it's very worth it to be a happier and healthier person. It's also important to remember that sexual abuse is not the victim's fault. I have had to explain this to many people over the years. Again, it's a normal feeling or thought that many people carry around, but those thoughts and feelings can be changed.

Sexual Abuse Prevention

If you want to take this topic to the next level, this section looks at what works towards preventing child sexual abuse. This was the topic of my dissertation and these were the findings. In her 1994 study, Daro (1994) concludes that prevention programs overall have beneficial impacts, which are strongest for children seven to twelve years old. She concludes with suggestions for expanding prevention efforts to include public and parent education, life skills training for young adults, support groups for vulnerable children and adults, and intervention for identified victims and perpetrators.

One of the most consistent recommendations from the evaluations is the need to provide children with opportunities for role-play to practice new skills such as assertiveness, clear communication, and maintaining a safe distance from strangers. Wurtele and Miller-Perrin (1992) found role-playing and participant modeling, such as actively practicing a skill as opposed to watching others do it, a more effective method than experimenter modeling of prevention skills. In response, child safety programs are increasingly utilizing this technique.

Fryer et al. (1997) concluded that there is retention for those who have mastered this, and that there is value in re-teaching skills for those who have failed. They also noted a need to continue research to further evolve the program. Since this was conducted in the late 1980s, it would be critical to add an online component to subsequent programs (Fryer et al., 1987). Repetition apparently strengthens the likelihood for success. In this sense, the initial presentation of safety concepts and skills in preschool settings may establish a critical foundation for later learning (Gilbert, 1989).

One initiative was conducted in Minnesota from 2002-2007. The program involved obtaining a grant and support from the state with the goal to educate on and prevent child sexual abuse on a macro and micro level. They were able to educate via presentations to adults, children, and professionals who work with children. They developed partnerships with other agencies and organizations, as well as the media. They also provided testimony to the state-level commission on sex offender policy that resulted in recommendations for focusing on prevention. The results were an increase in adult action to prevent child sexual abuse, as evidenced by an increase in calls to the Stop It Now! hotline with a focus on preventive reporting. There was also a reduction in the reported occurrences of child sexual abuse in Minnesota (Schober et al., 2008).

The SAIT study focused on adult participants' knowledge about rape, empathy for rape victims, and reducing the acceptance for myths about rape. This was done through pre and post-tests assessing knowledge and myth acceptance. There were also empathy for victim exercises done through discussions of videos. One of the noteworthy results was in the use of the pre-test. It is believed that completing a pre-test highlights what the learner needs to focus on during the learning. As a result, there was an improvement in scores from beginning to end (Rau et al., 2011).

Recent studies with randomized assignment to different treatment conditions indicate that session-limited cognitive behavioral therapy is effective for some symptoms in sexually abused children. Deblinger et al. (1996) compared 100 sexually abused children randomized to four treatment conditions. These conditions were a twelve-week abuse-focused cognitive behavioral therapy model for the child only, cognitive behavioral therapy for the parent only, cognitive behavioral therapy for both parent and child, and standardized community care. They found that all groups improved, but cognitive behavioral therapy provided directly to the child resulted in the most benefit.

Cohen and Mannarino (1998) included a non-offending parent in both the cognitive behavioral therapy and non-directive supportive therapy components. In one study of three to sevenyear-olds, children receiving cognitive behavioral therapy showed significant improvement in post-traumatic stress disorder symptoms and internalizing, externalizing, and sexually inappropriate behaviors that were sustained over one year. Overall, abuse-focused cognitive behavioral therapy models provided to the child along with similar treatment to a non-offending parent are currently some of the best-documented, effective treatments for child sexual abuse.

I work extensively with sexual offenders and we, as a society, put a lot of resources into supervising and treating perpetrators of sexual abuse. As noted before, 95% of sexual offenses are committed by someone who isn't known as a sex offender. I have a colleague from our local CAC (Child Advocacy Center) who often says we put 95% of our resources into 5% of the problem. That's a bit disproportionate. There are a number of great programs and resources that work towards prevention.

Education and prevention of child sexual abuse are critical to protecting children and fostering safe environments. Effective strategies involve raising awareness, teaching children about body safety, training adults to recognize and respond to signs of abuse, and implementing policies that support child protection. Below are key approaches to education and prevention.

Education for Children

Body Safety Education
Teach Consent: Educate children about the concept of consent and their right to say no to unwanted touches.

Appropriate and Inappropriate Touch: Help children understand the difference between appropriate and inappropriate touch.

Private Parts: Use age-appropriate language to teach children that certain parts of their body are private and should not be touched by others.

Empowerment and Communication
Encourage Open Communication: Foster an environment where children feel comfortable talking about their feelings and experiences.

Assertiveness Training: Teach children to assertively say no and to seek help from trusted adults if they feel uncomfortable.

Safety Rules
Safe and Unsafe Secrets: Explain the difference between safe and unsafe secrets, emphasizing that it's okay to tell a trusted adult if they feel uncomfortable.

Identify Trusted Adults: Help children identify who they can turn to if they need help, such as parents, teachers, or other trusted adults.

Education for Adults

Recognizing Signs of Abuse
Behavioral Indicators: Teach adults the behavioral signs of sexual abuse, such as sudden changes in behavior, regression, or inappropriate sexual behavior.

Physical Indicators: Educate adults about physical signs, including unexplained injuries or discomfort in the genital area.

Responding to Disclosure
Listen and Believe: Encourage adults to listen carefully and believe children when they disclose abuse.

Reassurance and Support: Teach adults to reassure the child that they did the right thing by telling and assure them that they are not to blame.

Report and Follow-Up: Instruct adults on how to report suspected abuse to the appropriate authorities and ensure the child receives necessary support.

Preventive Measures
Supervision: Emphasize the importance of adequate supervision in settings where children are present.

Safe Environment: Create and maintain environments that minimize opportunities for abuse, such as clear policies and physical safeguards in schools and organizations.

Training Programs

Professional Development

Mandatory Training: Implement mandatory training for educators, childcare providers, healthcare professionals, and other individuals working with children.

Ongoing Education: Provide continuous education and refresher courses to keep professionals updated on best practices and new information.

Parental Education

Workshops and Seminars: Offer workshops and seminars for parents to educate them about child sexual abuse, prevention strategies, and how to talk to their children about body safety.

Resources and Support: Provide resources such as books, online courses, and support groups for parents.

Community Involvement

Public Awareness Campaigns

Media Campaigns: Utilize media to raise awareness about child sexual abuse and promote prevention strategies.

Community Events: Host community events, such as safety fairs or educational forums, to engage the public and provide information.

Policy and Advocacy

Child Protection Policies: Advocate for and implement strong child protection policies in schools, organizations, and communities.

Legislation: Support legislation that strengthens protections for children and mandates reporting and training.

Collaboration

Interagency Cooperation: Encourage collaboration between schools, law enforcement, healthcare providers, and child protective services to create a coordinated response to child sexual abuse.

Community Networks: Build networks of organizations and individuals dedicated to preventing child sexual abuse and supporting victims.

Resources and Support

Hotlines and Helplines

National and Local Helplines: Ensure that children and adults have access to hotlines where they can report abuse and seek help. There's more info in the resource section.

Confidential Support: Provide confidential support and resources for victims and their families.

Therapeutic Services

Counseling and Therapy: Offer access to counseling and therapeutic services for victims of abuse and their families.

Support Groups: Create support groups for survivors of child sexual abuse to share their experiences and receive peer support.

Preventing child sexual abuse requires a comprehensive approach that includes education, awareness, and proactive measures. By empowering children with knowledge, training adults to recognize and respond to signs of abuse, and fostering supportive communities, we can create safer environments and reduce the incidence of child sexual abuse. Collaboration among families, schools, organizations, and policymakers is essential to ensure the safety and well-being of all children.

There are a number of accredited sexual abuse prevention programs available to schools and community groups. Despite the clear benefits of education and prevention programs, it was difficult to get the programs into schools as sexual abuse is a provocative and sensitive topic. To help alleviate this, Erin's Law has been enacted into law in over thirty states. Erin Merryn was a victim of sexual abuse who has dedicated her life to promoting education and prevention programs into law. There are links to a number of accredited prevention programs in the resource section.

Chapter 12

START BEING THE BEST
VERSION OF YOURSELF

"I choose to live by choice, not by chance; to make changes,
not excuses; to be motivated, not manipulated; to be
useful, not used; to excel, not to compete. I choose self-
esteem, not self-pity. I choose to listen to my inner voice,
not the random opinion of others. I choose to be me."
– Miranda Marrott

Earlier, we discussed the ideal self, based on Carl Rogers' theories. Now, we'll flesh that out. One way to start is by looking at our role models. Some people say they had no good role models. I used to conduct group therapy in boarding houses in a crime-ridden area. While driving through the neighborhood, I would see houses with play sets on the front lawn and I would be sad for the families, especially the children, who lived there. It seemed like they were starting from a huge disadvantage. In getting to know some of the stories, I saw many hard-working parents trying to provide the best they could for their children. The more resilient factors present, the better the chances.

When it comes to role models, it's ideal to have them at home. Even then, some people choose negative ones and blame it on a lack of options. That's an excuse, not a reason. Years ago, Stan Lee had a TV show called "Who Wants to be a Superhero?" One of the contestants told Stan that he'd raised him, even though they had never met. The contestant went on to explain that his father had passed away when he was young, and he grew up without a father. He read a lot of comic books and felt like they were written directly to him. The comic books focused a lot on the qualities and morals of heroes, and he developed his ideal self from those messages.

Messages and models are everywhere–good and bad. I find it's good to see them in different people in various settings and embody them. I've met and seen many great people in my life and have purposely taken different parts and characteristics from many of them. For example, one of my first college professors had a two-handed handshake where you felt his genuineness. I've been trying to copy it ever since then. I haven't mastered it, but I'm still working on it.

Role models don't have to be perfect. No one is. They just have to have qualities that we can add to our list. The reality is everyone is flawed. The cool thing is when you accept this statement. If you accept that you are flawed, you should become more patient with other people's flaws. There can be an inner peace in this acceptance. So if I'm flawed, how can I become my ideal self? You never fully can. That's part of the acceptance of flaws. This idea should not be an excuse to not do the work to get there.

If you want to take that concept to the next level, think about people you don't like so much. Instead of focusing on their flaws, focus on their strengths or positive qualities. It's not as easy, but when you're able to do it, your overall lens improves dramatically. Interestingly, the people who annoy us the most, are usually reflective of things we don't like about ourselves. In psychology, it's called projection. As with most of our problems, it's not about them, it's about us.

When thinking about role models, it's about qualities, not things. Sometimes we have the quality in mind and then see someone do it well. Other times, we may not have a quality in mind until we see it and it makes an impact. One of my most influential role models has always been Arnold Schwarzenegger. When I started lifting weights, Arnold was the natural influence, but there was much more to it. He was also extremely smart and goal-driven. I read everything he wrote over the years and have always found inspiration. I've never met him and am sure he has flaws, but I am grateful for the positive ways he has influenced me.

If you don't have any role models and are thinking about how to apply the ideal self concept, think about the qualities that you want to possess or embody. I have this conversation with many of the groups I work with, and the conversation is usually the same. Keep in mind, my groups often consist of individuals who are from various demographic groups with many differences and many similarities. They've also committed various crimes, and many have led that lifestyle for years. I ask them to think about their ideal selves, and the values that come up are often very similar to each other. Interestingly, their list is very similar to the list that anyone reading this book would come up with.

How can criminals have the same ideal value system as non-criminals? That's where the conversations get interesting. Many people choose the wrong role models or examples and use them as an excuse. With that said, many people really may have bad examples early on and this can stifle emotional development. It's all fixable by realizing this and choosing better examples or values.

Positive values are core beliefs and principles that guide behavior, decision-making, and interactions with others. They are essential for personal development, building healthy relationships, and creating a fulfilling life. Below are some key positive values and their significance.

Integrity, which involves -
Honesty: Being truthful and transparent in your actions and communications.
Trustworthiness: Being reliable and dependable, earning the trust of others through consistent and ethical behavior.

Respect, which involves -
Respect for Others: Valuing the dignity and worth of all individuals, treating them with kindness and consideration.

Self-Respect: Maintaining a healthy sense of self-worth and setting boundaries that protect your well-being.

Responsibility, which involves -

Accountability: Taking responsibility for your actions and their consequences, and owning up to mistakes.

Dependability: Being reliable and consistent in fulfilling commitments and obligations.

Compassion, which involves -

Empathy: Understanding and sharing the feelings of others, and responding with kindness and support.

Altruism: Acting selflessly to help others, often putting their needs before your own.

Fairness, which involves -

Justice: Treating others equitably and making decisions based on fairness and equality.

Open-Mindedness: Being willing to consider different perspectives and ideas without bias.

Courage, which involves -

Bravery: Facing challenges, risks, and fears with strength and determination.

Perseverance: Staying committed to your goals despite obstacles and setbacks.

Humility, which involves -

Modesty: Recognizing your limitations and being humble about your achievements.

Gratitude: Appreciating what you have and expressing thanks for the kindness and support of others.

Generosity, which involves -

Giving: Willingly sharing your time, resources, and talents to help others.

Kindness: Performing acts of kindness and showing compassion and concern for others.

Loyalty, which involves -

Faithfulness: Being loyal and committed to your relationships, principles, and responsibilities.

Supporting: Standing by and supporting others, especially during difficult times.

Optimism, which involves -

Positive Outlook: Maintaining a hopeful and positive attitude, even in the face of challenges.

Resilience: Bouncing back from adversity and maintaining a sense of hope and determination.

Honesty, which involves -

Sincerity: Being genuine and authentic in your interactions, without deceit or pretense.

Transparency: Being open and clear about your intentions, actions, and decisions.

Patience, which involves -

Tolerance: Being patient and understanding with others, especially in difficult or frustrating situations.

Endurance: Having the patience to persist through challenges and wait for the right opportunities.

Discipline, which involves -

Self-Control: Exercising control over your impulses and emotions, making thoughtful and deliberate decisions.

Consistency: Maintaining a steady and consistent approach to your goals and responsibilities.

Forgiveness, which involves -

Letting Go of Grudges: Forgiving others for their mistakes and moving forward without holding on to resentment.

Self-Forgiveness: Allowing yourself to move past your own mistakes and learn from them without self-condemnation.

Innovation, which involves -

Creativity: Embracing new ideas, thinking outside the box, and being open to change and innovation.

Curiosity: Maintaining a sense of wonder and a desire to learn and explore new things.

Positive values serve as the foundation for a meaningful and ethical life. They guide your behavior, influence your decisions, and shape your relationships with others. By embodying and practicing these values, you can build a life of integrity, compassion, and fulfillment. This is a comprehensive list, and each one speaks differently to each of us. You probably emotionally relate to many of them, and may even feel you already live them. The point of this exercise is to identify and improve.

For example, it's important to me to be positive. That means I strive towards positive thinking and challenge negative thoughts. Earlier, we discussed how thoughts lead to feelings, which then lead to behaviors. By focusing on positive thoughts, I am carrying that to feelings and actions. As good as I try to be, I am consistently aware in order to evolve and not fall backwards. It can be argued that negative can be fun sometimes, but it takes me away from my ideal self.

As you consciously pick the values that speak to you, picture what that means and what it looks like when you do it. If you're always checking yourself, how can you be happy? Knowing that you are constantly working on you is the reward, as you will continually be becoming a better you. Think of it as physical exercise. When are you ever done? You're not, but if you have healthy physical habits, you are constantly improving your physical and mental health. If you don't, you run a higher risk of health problems, have lower serotonin levels, and know that you aren't taking care of yourself.

There are days when it's tough to get motivated to exercise. Most of the time, our reasons for not exercising are excuses, not reasons. It's rare that you leave the gym or track and say I shouldn't have done that. My motto for myself is, "When in doubt, work out." This means if I question whether I should work out, the answer is automatically yes. As a result, I haven't missed a week at the gym since I was fourteen. The exception was COVID, where I had to use a makeshift home gym. This is where role models come in to give us a push. Arnold has a two-minute clip online where he talks about time management and not making excuses that keep you from your goals.

Ultimately, if we aren't behaving in a way that is consistent with our values, we can't be fully happy. This may happen on an unconscious level, and that's when our defense mechanisms kick in to make us feel better. They're almost like the devil on your shoulder saying that it's okay to make the wrong choice. If you're not familiar with Freud's defense mechanisms, here is a quick lesson.

Sigmund Freud's defense mechanisms are psychological strategies used by the unconscious mind to protect an individual from anxiety and the stress arising from unacceptable thoughts or feelings. These mechanisms often distort reality in some way to reduce psychological tension. Below are some of Freud's key defense mechanisms.

Repression
Definition: Repression involves unconsciously blocking unacceptable thoughts, feelings, and memories from conscious awareness.

Example: A person who experienced a traumatic event in childhood may not have any conscious memory of it, but the repressed memory can influence their behavior and emotions.

Denial
Definition: Denial is the refusal to accept reality or facts, acting as if a painful event, thought, or feeling does not exist.

Example: A person who is a heavy smoker may deny the evidence linking smoking to serious health issues, insisting that smoking is not harmful.

Projection

Definition: Projection involves attributing one's own unacceptable thoughts, feelings, or impulses to another person.

Example: A person who is angry with their boss may instead believe that their boss is angry with them.

Displacement

Definition: Displacement shifts emotional reactions from the original source of distress to a safer or more acceptable substitute target.

Example: After a frustrating day at work, a person may come home and take out their anger on their family instead of confronting their boss.

Regression

Definition: Regression involves reverting to behaviors or characteristics of an earlier stage of development when faced with stress or anxiety.

Example: An adult might throw a temper tantrum or exhibit childish behaviors when they are under significant stress.

Sublimation

Definition: Sublimation is the channeling of unacceptable impulses into socially acceptable or constructive activities.

Example: A person with aggressive tendencies may take up a sport like boxing or become a surgeon, where these impulses can be expressed in a controlled and socially approved manner.

Rationalization

Definition: Rationalization involves creating a seemingly logical reason or explanation for behavior that might otherwise be shameful or unacceptable.

Example: A student who fails an exam might blame the teacher's poor instruction rather than their own lack of preparation.

Reaction Formation

Definition: Reaction formation involves behaving in a way that is opposite to one's unacceptable impulses.

Example: A person who feels insecure about their sexuality might adopt a very homophobic stance to hide their true feelings.

Identification

Definition: Identification involves adopting the characteristics or behaviors of another person, often someone who is seen as a role model or authority figure.

Example: A young boy might emulate his father's mannerisms and values to deal with feelings of inadequacy.

Intellectualization

Definition: Intellectualization involves using reasoning and logic to block out emotional stress and feelings.

Example: A person who is diagnosed with a terminal illness might focus on learning about the disease and its treatment options, rather than addressing the emotional impact of the diagnosis.

Compensation

Definition: Compensation involves making up for perceived deficiencies or feelings of inferiority in one area by excelling in another.

Example: Someone who feels they are not academically gifted might put all their efforts into excelling in sports.

Freud's defense mechanisms illustrate how individuals unconsciously cope with anxiety and internal conflict. Understanding these mechanisms can provide insight into behaviors and emotional responses, both in oneself and others. While these mechanisms can be protective and adaptive, they can also become maladaptive if overused or relied upon excessively, potentially leading to psychological issues. Remember, if you own it, you can fix it. Defense mechanisms are less needed as you become a better you and don't need to unconsciously protect yourself from yourself.

If you haven't done it yet, take out your notes and write, "My Ideal Self", and create your ideal self. Write down the values and behaviors that embody who you want to be. This is your destination. It's important to be clear with yourself with how you want to be so you can check yourself along the way. It won't feel natural for a little while, and you'll be acting out the behaviors until they become natural.

Consider the behaviors you want to apply as habits. Good or bad, habits are developed over time. Developing positive habits is essential for personal growth, productivity, and overall well-being. Below are some steps and strategies to help you develop and maintain positive habits.

Identify Your Goals

Define Your Why: Understand why you want to develop a specific habit. Knowing the underlying reason can motivate you to stick with it.

Set Clear Goals: Make your goals specific, measurable, achievable, relevant, and time-bound (SMART).

Start Small

Small Steps: Begin with small, manageable steps that can be easily incorporated into your daily routine.

Focus on One Habit at a Time: Trying to change too many habits at once can be overwhelming. Focus on one habit until it becomes ingrained.

Create a Routine

Consistency: Practice the habit at the same time and in the same context each day to build consistency.

Daily Reminders: Use reminders, such as alarms, notes, or apps, to prompt you to perform the habit.

Make It Enjoyable

Positive Association: Associate the habit with something enjoyable. For example, listening to your favorite music while exercising.

Reward Yourself: Reward yourself after completing the habit to create a positive reinforcement loop.

Track Your Progress

Habit Tracker: Use a habit tracker app or a journal to record your progress and stay motivated.

Reflect and Adjust: Regularly review your progress, reflect on what's working, and adjust your approach as needed.

Overcome Obstacles

Identify Barriers: Recognize potential obstacles that might hinder your progress and plan strategies to overcome them.

Stay Flexible: Be prepared to adapt and find alternative ways to maintain the habit if challenges arise.

Build a Support System

Accountability Partner: Find a friend or family member who can hold you accountable and provide encouragement.

Join a Community: Join groups or communities with similar goals to share experiences and support each other.

Use Habit Stacking

Anchor New Habits: Attach the new habit to an existing habit to make it easier to remember. For example, meditate right after brushing your teeth.

Create Routines: Build routines that incorporate multiple positive habits together.

Practice Patience and Persistence

Be Patient: Understand that developing new habits takes time. Be patient with yourself and allow time for the habit to become ingrained.

Stay Persistent: Don't get discouraged by setbacks. Keep pushing forward and recommit to your goals after any slip-ups.

Self-Reflection and Adaptation

Self-Reflection: Regularly reflect on your progress, challenges, and successes. Use this insight to stay motivated and make necessary adjustments.

Adapt and Evolve: As you grow and your circumstances change, be willing to adapt your habits to continue supporting your goals.

Focus on the Long Term

Lifestyle Integration: Think of habit formation as a long-term lifestyle change rather than a short-term goal.

Intrinsic Motivation: Develop habits that are intrinsically rewarding and align with your values and passions.

Examples of Positive Habits

Exercise: Incorporate regular physical activity into your routine, whether it's a daily walk, yoga, or gym workouts.

Healthy Eating: Develop healthy eating habits by planning balanced meals and avoiding processed foods.

Reading: Set aside time each day for reading to expand your knowledge and stimulate your mind.

Mindfulness and Meditation: Practice mindfulness or meditation to reduce stress and increase mental clarity.

Hydration: Make a habit of drinking enough water throughout the day to stay hydrated and support overall health.

Time Management: Use tools and techniques to manage your time effectively and stay organized.

Developing positive habits requires intention, consistency, and perseverance. By setting clear goals, starting small, tracking progress, and building a supportive environment, you can successfully integrate positive habits into your daily life. Remember that the journey to habit formation is ongoing, and staying flexible and patient will help you achieve lasting change. It's actually a lot easier than it sounds. It just takes conscious thought until it's unconscious. For long-term relationships to have the best chance of working, both people need to be in a good place with themselves. After all, how can we love someone else if we don't love ourselves? We've worked on the "you" part, now let's look at applying it to relationships.

Chapter 13

DEVELOPING AND MAINTAINING HEALTHY RELATIONSHIPS

My primary relationship is with myself, all others are mirrors of it. As I learn to love myself, I automatically receive the love and appreciation that I desire from others. If I am committed to myself and to living my truth, I will attract others with equal commitment. My willingness to be intimate with my own deep feelings creates the space for intimacy with another. As I learn to love myself, I receive the love I desire from others.
– Shakti Gawain

We've arrived at our last chapter. Hopefully, you've used this book to consciously and deliberately rebuild yourself while leaving the unnecessary baggage behind. The most important relationship we each have is with ourselves. Now, we'll focus on developing relationships with others who have, hopefully, done the same.

Marry the parent that you like

Huh?

This is one of my favorite quotes from a colleague of mine many years ago. It is based on Freudian psychology, where we all marry our parents. No one likes the idea of this, but it happens too much to be dismissed. You may think you are the exception, which is why you wrote the lists in the last chapter.

We're now going to do one of my favorite exercises that I use in therapy sessions. I really want you to take the time to do this as it's going to be really helpful. Take out a piece of paper. You can also type, if you prefer. We'll base this on two parents. If you grew up with a single parent, you may base it on one. Ultimately, you're going to base your list on who primarily raised you. For each person, make two lists – the positive qualities of that person and the negative qualities.

Since we are strongly influenced, both consciously and unconsciously, by our parent influences, it's important to take the steps to choose the influence they have on our current and future relationships. This is another concept that Freud had a lot of insight on. Think about past relationships and it's likely that the negative qualities of past partners matched many of the negative qualities you just listed. It didn't happen by accident. We're drawn to what we know. The best way to break that pattern is to seek the positive we're used to and avoid the negative that we're used to. Earlier in the book, we looked at keeping the good from our past and leaving the bad. To maximize your relationship future, use this list as a checklist to marry the parent that you like. Ultimately, that means they will likely be a combination of the best of your influences.

If you're in a relationship, let's see how your partner checks out by doing a positive and negative list on them. You may or may not want to share this list with your significant other, as the negative quality list can be quite controversial. This is especially true when comparing it to your parent list. If you have been with your significant other for a while, then the list should not be surprising. What should stand out right away is whose negative qualities they may have. For example, my mother has always been clumsy and has broken many coffee pots over the years. We have a Keurig coffee maker, so my wife just breaks glasses or spills her coffee. This only fits in the negative list as it gets expensive, and she tends to break glasses that I like.

As you go through the list, hopefully there are more positive qualities drawn out from both of your parents. If that is not the case, and the majority of similarities are from the negative qualities you grew up with, then it is time to reflect. Not every negative is horrible, i.e., clumsiness. However, some negative qualities are very bad, such as abusive behavior, alcoholism, or cheating. This may be all you know, but it doesn't have to be all you will ever know.

If you aren't in a relationship, you may be wondering how this applies to you. This is the perfect time for you to be reading this book. When you write the list, it should be based on your most recent relationship(s). By doing this, you can see who you've been looking for in a partner. If your past partner was reflective of the positive qualities you grew up with, then it is time to look at the list of yourself and see where you fit.

I had a patient in her early thirties come to therapy to sort out her pattern of dysfunctional relationships. The first thing I had her do was to break up with the married man she was with. Once she "cleaned out her house", she was able to look around and figure things out. No relationship is better than an unhealthy one. She was then able to clearly look at her past relationships and see which parents she was marrying. From there, she was able to choose a healthy person as well as identify people who were unhealthy. That was about two years ago and she is currently engaged to get married to a guy with the good qualities she grew up with instead of the bad ones.

What do you need?

Patterns are very common for people to follow. Some do this consciously and some do it unconsciously. It is sad when people have negative patterns and can't seem to break from them. Part of the reason for this is because of the concept of needs. Needs are things that we can't live without. Remember when we talked about Abraham Maslow? Maslow introduced the concept of the hierarchy of needs. The premise is that human beings behave in a way to get their needs met. Maslow suggested that there is an order that this occurs in. If someone's lower needs aren't met, then they can't pursue meeting their higher ones.

Lower needs are basic needs like food, clothing and shelter. This is followed by physical and emotional safety. Higher level needs include belongingness, self-esteem, and self-actualization. If someone is hungry or homeless, it is difficult for them to think about developing their self-esteem.

Even though there is a lot of value to this concept, there is another way to look at needs which is more open-ended. Needs have to be met, and we behave in a way to meet them, but there doesn't have to be an order. With that in mind, we can look at everything we do and attach it to a need. For example, someone may exercise because it feels good and meets a need for self-esteem. Someone else may use drugs for the same reason. The need is the same, but the behavior is different. If the person using drugs wants to stop because it is a negative behavior, they have to find a new behavior to meet that need.

Relationships work the same way. We often choose to be in relationships to meet the needs of belongingness and self-esteem. When someone picks an unhealthy or abusive relationship and stays, it is an attempt to feel connected to someone (belongingness). The problem is they are seeking to get their needs met through someone else instead of doing it from within first. It is very difficult to love another person if you don't love yourself first.

In the 90s, there was a movie called "Jerry Maguire" where Renée Zellweger's character told Tom Cruise's character, "You complete me." Women swooned, and it became one of the most romantic lines to tell someone. It's actually one of the most ridiculous and co-dependent statements one can make. For someone to complete us, we would have to be incomplete. If we can't be complete without another person, we are dependent on them to be whole. Clinically speaking, we should be a complete person before we look to be with someone else. The ideal situation is for two complete people to choose to be together.

The common theme throughout this book is self-love. This can only happen as you work towards your ideal self. That is only possible when you've resolved your past issues that might be keeping you from that goal. The question to be asked is, when do you know you are a complete person who is ready to be in a healthy relationship? The next question is, how do you know if someone else is ready? The answer to both questions is easy. It begins with a life score.

What is a life score?

In psychological assessment, we have something called a global assessment of functioning. It is a score from 0-100 meant to identify what a person's current level of functioning is. Some of the factors involved are looking at where someone is in terms of work, relationships, and emotional functioning. In therapy, I simplify it by calling it a life score. At any given time in life, we have a life score, but it goes up and down depending on where we are. The more stable you are with employment, healthy relationships, and healthy decision-making, the higher your score should be.

The life score is a great way to measure where we've been, where we are, and where we want to go. It is also a great way to measure our compatibility with another person. Here are some points to consider when looking at this concept:

- If you were a 30 and moved up to a 50, that is great, but it probably isn't your goal score. The problem is, if you are at a 50, you will probably end up with another 50.
- It should go without saying, but two 50s do not make 100.
- You may want an 80, but why would an 80 be with a 50?
- If you go for someone with a lower score, that will not help to bring your score up. In fact, it will most likely serve to bring your score down.
- You should get to a healthy and comfortable score before looking to be with someone.

The Starbucks Girl

One of my former clients had the best insight into this concept. I'll use the name "Dave" for discussion purposes. In the past, he would look for "strippers and porn stars". He had a very sordid past (including many years in jail) so there was some compatibility. He realized his past pattern always led to the same outcome, which included unhealthy places and decisions. At the time, he was a 30 at best. When he initially spoke about wanting a Starbucks girl, he was still a 30. He said he wanted to change his pattern to be with a Starbucks girl. A Starbucks girl is a girl who has a job, her own place, her own car, and can afford a five dollar cup of coffee. He also said that he knew he had no business looking for a Starbucks girl until he became a Starbucks guy.

You may be reading this in a Starbucks and feel that you've made it. It's good that you can be there, but it doesn't necessarily mean that the work is done. Dave went from being in prison to homeless, then he worked his way up to the point of having his own place, car, job, and he could go to Starbucks and get his five dollar cup of coffee. Unfortunately, he never dealt with his past issues, relapsed on drugs, and returned to prison. Logically, he knew what it meant to get to a better score, but he tried the usual shortcuts of saying the right thing but never really talking about anything. He did raise his score in some areas, but not as many as he needed. So how do you know if someone else is ready?

Red flags and rules of engagement

People often ignore red flags that appear early on in relationships. We do this by downplaying or dismissing behaviors or concerns that we experience. Some red flags may be reacting strongly in simple situations, excessive drinking, lying, shouting, extreme secrecy, etc. There are a lot of reasons why people do this. Some feel addressing these issues may drive the person away. Some people feel we all have our issues, so we should not judge. Often, the person apologizes and promises not to do it again, so they are forgiven. Not surprisingly, when relationships fail, those early red flags are usually a big part of the break-up. Unfortunately, there may have been a lot of hurt before that happens.

Red flags should not be ignored. They don't have to be deal-breakers but should be explored and taken seriously. When my wife and I started dating, we were in our 20s. We had our first argument, and she started yelling and cursing. This is not uncommon for people when they argue. For me, it was uncommon, as that hadn't happened to me. I told her that I won't yell and curse and that I don't want to be yelled or cursed at. The next thing I said was the most important. I said, "I don't want to be in a relationship where it is okay to speak to each other that way. Do you?" She paused for a moment and said that she didn't want that either. Once we decided it's not okay, we had to agree on how we did want to communicate.

That approach worked because it moved her from an emotional state to a logical one. Remember this concept from before? It's difficult to have a meaningful conversation or resolution when one or both people are acting on emotion. When you think about it logically, why would you want it to be okay to yell and curse at someone you are supposed to care about? When people say they are okay with it, the reason is usually not the healthiest. In reality, most couples that do yell and curse usually didn't start that way. Over time, they crossed little lines and don't know how to go back once they have. The best way to uncross a line is to not cross it in the first place.

We decided that we didn't want that to be our dynamic so we made a mutual agreement to not yell or curse, especially when we argue. We agreed on a couple of other items and called it our rules of engagement. Our rules of engagement are:

- no yelling
- no cursing
- no sarcasm
- no family

Sarcasm can be traced back to the Greek verb, *sarkazein*, which initially meant "to tear flesh like a dog." It is often used in a similar way today, especially when people are emotional. In arguments, sarcasm is often insulting and biting with a smile, or smirk. It can be very funny, but is ultimately meant to hurt. Bringing up family in an argument can escalate things very quickly, i.e., "you're being like your mother."

You can learn a lot about a person during arguments. People often see it as a green light to say whatever they want, however they want to say it. These are not nice or healthy thoughts or behaviors. People often do this because they feel hurt or vulnerable. When someone is hurt, it is natural to want to hurt back. If you have been doing things this way for your whole life, it is difficult to change it. Here is a simple rule to help change it–you can't unsay what you say, therefore, think before you speak.

The Interview

When looking to be with someone long-term, it is important to go in with eyes wide open. I always advise my clients to interview the other person as well as have them interview you. Earlier, we discussed being a complete person first. A complete person can talk about their stuff. Someone who is not in a good place with their past has a hard time talking about it. If someone won't talk about it, then it is still part of their present.

People often avoid the interview because they don't want to answer certain questions, so they won't ask them of someone else. Here are some questions that people should be able to answer:

- What are you looking for in a relationship?

Many times, people are not on the same page with what they want. This is all part of putting everything on the table. If both people want to have a casual and open relationship, that is fine. If only one does, then it's not going to work. The same is true for a committed relationship.

- What are some reasons past relationships have not worked out?

If there is a pattern of drama, abuse, or cheating, then logic would suggest the pattern will continue. The exception to this is if the person can say what the pattern was and what they've done to change it. If they've really worked on it, then they are able to talk about it. If they are defensive, they may still have some work to do.

- What is your history with drugs and alcohol?

Everyone has different feelings about this issue, and people are usually more tolerant in the beginning. Drug and alcohol abuse is a huge factor and multiple relapses are common. This problem extends to prescription drugs as well. Not every prescription drug is bad, but if someone has been on painkillers or drugs like Xanax for years, that is a red flag.

- What is your relationship with your family?

As discussed earlier, Freudian psychology is alive and well. It is said, look how a guy talks to his mother and that's how he'll talk to his wife. The same goes for females. People often look to resolve their parental issues through their relationship choices. I had a client recently say he chose a mother figure as his mother was so involved in drugs when he was growing up, that she was never really there. He is still looking for the mother he never had.

If someone is completely isolated from their family, that is a red flag. A friend in my firehouse said that every family has someone who is screwed up. If you can't figure out who it is, then it is probably you. If you think everyone in your family is screwed up, then it's probably still you. Some people have the opposite problem, as they are too ingrained with their family. An adult is able to make decisions on their own without having their family involved in every decision. Again, this can be a red flag.

- How do you handle your finances?

My wife and I both had horrible credit scores when we started dating. We were in our twenties and were still learning financial responsibility. We discussed this openly and developed better habits. As a result, our credit scores are much better. It took many years, but we did it together. Finances are one of the main issues in divorce. If a couple cannot be open, honest, and responsible regarding finances, then the prognosis is not good. If this is an area you can relate to and want to improve in it, please see the resource list for *The Couple's Guide to Love and Money* by one of my inspiring professors, Jonathan Rich, Ph.D. The book really takes this idea and helps a couple work through one of the biggest causes of divorce.

Putting it all together

By now, you should have all the pieces necessary to make a healthy and informed decision. Start with the list you made of your partner. Put it next to the lists of your parents. Check off each positive from your partner list that appears on either parent positive list. Add the number of checks. Also, take note of which parent list has more checks. That is the positive you are looking to repeat, and that is the parent that taught it to you.

Now do the same thing for the negative lists. This is where your problem is. This shows you what qualities you have been carrying with you and where you learned them. This is the least comfortable list to accept. Since they are qualities of another person (your partner), you cannot change it and you can't blame them. You chose this. Hopefully, the pros outweigh the cons. You'll know this by adding the checks from both lists and seeing which is higher. Statistically speaking, there are a number of people reading this that should realize the cons outweigh the pros. So, what do you do?

If you are with the parent you don't like (the negative list outweighs the positive), you have some decisions to make. The most proactive thing to do is to share this with your partner and have an open discussion about what it means. You may be afraid to do this, but it is fairer than just ending it and more healthy than doing nothing. Besides, you may be rating high in their list too.

If you are not in a relationship and are just reflecting on past ones, you are in a very good place. You should be seeing your patterns and now know clearly what to look for. First, work on yourself. Second, be clear on the positive list and look for that in the next person. This is how you find the parent that you like.

If the pro list outweighs the con list, then you are probably with the parent that you like. Congratulations! It is possible to pick a healthy relationship and it is just that—a choice. Naturally, there is still work to do. There are probably some negatives checked off, so that is worth talking about but not obsessing on. For good or bad, you can't change another person. Therefore, you accept them as is and be grateful they are doing the same (remember the serenity prayer). My wife has some of the positives of both of my parents with very little of the negatives. We are happy and healthy and are teaching that to our children. When they get older, I'm sure they will have a list too.

Your 2 or 3 Adult Relationships

Author and psychotherapist Esther Perel says that, "In the West today, most people are going to have two or three marriages, two or three committed relationships in their adult life. It's just that some of us are going to do it with the same person." As someone who's been married for over twenty years, this concept really resonated with me and my wife. The concept is not based on time, it's based on a lot more. It's hard enough to be with ourselves for decades, let alone someone else.

We naturally change, hopefully, for the better, and there's no guarantee that two people will stay or grow closer. According to the CDC, the divorce rate in the United States is 42%. There are too many factors involved in breaking down why that is, but it doesn't have to be a complete negative. It's sad when a marriage doesn't last. It also doesn't mean that anyone failed. Sometimes, people just grow in different directions. Whenever there's a break-up, both people should take some time to play "What did I learn?" There are lessons to be learned in every relationship. If we don't reflect or if we just blame the other person, we are less likely to grow from the experience and are more prone to fall into cycles.

Break-ups don't have to have a good guy and a bad guy. It's sad when people reflect on relationships as total negatives and how terrible the other person was. This is often due to someone coping or grieving a loss, but they can lose the real moments that happened. Very often, the good moments were real. As people, our feelings constantly change. Our feelings about ourselves are often in flux, so our feelings about others can change as well. The two or three relationships we have are reflective of the stages in our life. It's not better or worse if that's with the same person or different people, it's just different paths.

When the next relationship is with the same person, that usually means that a shift has taken place. Often, that shift is due to being at a crossroads. A common cause is when both people realize they are at different points and have to reimagine the relationship. To do it right, this can be an intense process. It involves being vulnerable with each other about what's working and not working for each person. This is where all of the skills we discussed come into play. It's different from the start of the relationship, where discussions are based on past experiences. The learning is now drawn from the life you've lived together.

The positives are easy. You've done great things together and created great memories. The negatives are much harder. To evolve, you have to change things. Hearing what you've done that hasn't worked is difficult. It's rarely, if ever, one-sided. so both people have to be able to openly listen and commit to improving in different areas. This is where win-win is critical to success. The second relationship with the same person is, in some way, a new relationship with the same person, but better.

As Logan started college and Dylan was finishing high school, Christine and I went through this relationship metamorphosis. It took us several months to dig through twenty plus years of what was working, what wasn't working, what we needed to change, and what we needed to accept. We had developed some bad habits over the years, such as being overly sensitive at times and not speaking for days. We had to evolve to not be so sensitive. That means, realizing that many of the things we took offense to weren't intended to hurt. By not being so sensitive, you can laugh off many little incidents.

Taking a time-out from a tense situation is important. Not speaking for days is destructive. A time-out should be a brief period of time, maybe five minutes to an hour or so. Dragging that out creates an emotional divide that increases over time. It also causes us to snowball issues (think of the small snowball at the top of the hill getting bigger as it rolls down). Growing and evolving with someone throughout your life is fantastic, but it doesn't happen without constant communication, readjusting, and commitment to each other.

So, What's Next?

A goal without a plan is just a wish. Now that you've read the book, it's time to do the work. This means taking the time to plan and apply what you've learned. I've had many conversations with people who have spent many years in jail. Many of them reflected while they were in and did the work to make changes in their thinking and emotional management. I explain to them the thought process is the theoretical part, and being in the community and applying the change is the start of the work. Reflection and goals don't produce results without identifying the steps to get there and then taking action on them.

This book may have brought out issues you are not fully able to address on your own. If you don't do the work, you won't get there. It's like looking at the top of a mountain and wanting to get there, but not wanting to climb. You have to climb. If you do, you will get there, and you will be much better and happier for doing it. Use your support systems. Remember, there is strength in vulnerability. If you need extra support, see a therapist. Therapy doesn't have to be long-term. It can be focused and goal specific. You're never alone. If you ever need guidance, I'm there for you as well. Thank you for taking the time to read this book. You got this!

Resource List

Hotlines and Resources

CRISIS INTERVENTION 24/7 365 Care

- National Suicide Prevention Lifeline
  - 988lifeline.org – Online live chat
  - Call or Text 988

- Crisis Text Line
  - crisistextline.org – Online live chat
  - Text 741741

- Love Is Respect (Teen Dating Violence Hotline)
  - www.loveisrespect.org – Online Live Chat
  - Call 1.866.331.9474
  - Text LOVEIS (568347) to 22522

- National Domestic Violence Hotline
  - thehotline.org – Online live chat
  - Call 1.800.799.SAFE (7233)
  - Text START to 88788

- RAINN Rape, Abuse, Incest National Network
  - rainn.org – Online live chat
  - Call 1.800.656.HOPE (4673)

- SAMHSA Substance Abuse and Mental Health Services Administration
  - Call 1.800.662.HELP (4357)
  - findtreatment.gov

CHILD ABUSE & MALTREATMENT

- Child Help Hotline
  - childhelphotline.org – Online live chat
  - Call or Text 1.800.422.4453

- NCMEC National Center for Missing & Exploited Children
  - Call 1.800.THE.LOST (843-5678)
  - findtreatment.gov

- NCA National Children's Alliance
  - nationalchildrensalliance.org

- Prevent Child Abuse America
  - preventchildabuse.org

- Darkness To Light
  - d2l.org

- Enough Abuse
  - enoughabuse.org

- Erin's Law
  - erinslaw.org

- National Children's Advocacy Center
  - nationalcac.org

Please contact your local Department of Social Services Center for child abuse and maltreatment resources in your area.

DOMESTIC VIOLENCE

- National Domestic Violence Hotline
  - thehotline.org – Online live chat
  - Call 1.800.799.SAFE (7233)
  - Text START to 88788

- RAINN Rape, Abuse, Incest National Network
  - rainn.org – Online live chat
  - Call 1.800.656.HOPE (4673)

- Love Is Respect (Teen Dating Violence Hotline)
  - www.loveisrespect.org – Online Live Chat
  - Call 1.866.331.9474
  - Text LOVEIS (568347) to 22522

- NCADV National Coalition Against Domestic Violence
  - ncadv.org

- National Center on Domestic Violence, Trauma, and Mental Health
  - ncdvtmh.org

Please contact your local Department of Social Services Center for Domestic Violence Shelters in your area.

SUBSTANCE USE DISORDER

- SAMHSA Substance Abuse and Mental Health Services Administration
  - Call 1.800.662.HELP (4357)
  - findtreatment.gov

- Addiction Recovery Resources
  - Call 1.855.648.7728
  - recovered.org

- Substance Use Disorder Groups
  - aa.org – Alcoholics Anonymous
  - na.org – Narcotics Anonymous
  - al-anon.org – Al-Anon Family Groups

- NIDA National Institute on Drug Abuse
  - nida.nih.gov

- MAT Medication Assisted Treatment
  - samhsa.gov/medications-substance-use-disorders

ELDER ABUSE

- National Center on Elder Abuse
  - ncea.acl.gov

- Elder Justice Initiative
  - justice.gov/elderjustice

Please contact your local Department of Social Services Center for the Adult Protective Services in your area.

Printed in the United States
by Baker & Taylor Publisher Services